MW01698741

THE POCKET Ellen G. White DICTIONARY

MICHAEL W. CAMPBELL • JUD S. LAKE

Pacific Press®
Publishing Association
Nampa, Idaho | Oshawa, Ontario, Canada
www.pacificpress.com

Cover design by Gerald Lee Monks
Cover design resources from Darrel Tank
Inside design by Kristin Hansen-Mellish

Unless otherwise noted, all Scripture quotations are from the King James Version of the Bible.

The authors assume full responsibility for the accuracy of all facts and quotations as cited in this book.

Additional copies of this book are available by calling toll-free 1-800-765-6955 or by visiting http://www.AdventistBookCenter.com.

Library of Congress Cataloging-in-Publication Data
Names: Campbell, Michael W. (Teacher of Systematic Theology), author.
Title: The pocket Ellen G. White dictionary / Michael W. Campbell and Jud Lake.
Description: Nampa : Pacific Press Publishing Association, 2018. | Includes bibliographical references.
Identifiers: LCCN 2018014075 | ISBN 978-0-8163-6311-7 (pbk. : alk. paper)
Subjects: LCSH: White, Ellen Gould Harmon, 1827-1915—Dictionaries.
Classification: LCC BX6193.W5 C29 2018 | DDC 286.7092—dc23
LC record available at https://lccn.loc.gov/2018014075

March 2018

Dedication

To Jack Blanco, whose great admiration of and love for reading Ellen G. White's writings is contagious.

Other Books by Jud Lake

Ellen White Under Fire: Identifying the Mistakes of Her Critics

A Nation in God's Hands

Other Books by Michael W. Campbell

Discovering Ellen G. White

Discovering Our Adventist Past

Contents

Preface

This book fulfills the need to create a simple and ready reference work about the life and writings of Ellen G. White. The immediate impetus began as a result of teaching at the Adventist International Institute of Advanced Studies. Many non-native English-speaking students found some of Ellen White's words and expressions challenging. Furthermore, some of the terms were unfamiliar for individuals who were not from North America so even basic geographical terms were not familiar. Most of my students had never traveled to the United States. After assisting on *The Ellen G. White Encyclopedia* for more than a decade, my desire was to create a simple reference tool to look up basic words and key concepts. The goal was to develop something similar to what InterVarsity Press's academic imprint has done with a series of small reference works on church history, theology, and related topics. Thus, this book is a combination of both unusual words and expressions as well as a ready reference to key concepts, personalities, and historical events that were very much a part of Ellen G. White's life and world.

One of my close friends and former professors, Dr. Jud Lake, who has taught Adventist history and ministry for two decades at Southern Adventist University, gratefully contributed ideas and was willing to collaborate with me on this venture. The project has become much stronger than if either of us had ventured to do this on our own. We have had the opportunity to collaborate and tangibly share our mutual love for Adventist history and, specifically, our appreciation for the life and writings of Ellen G. White.

This is not intended to be a groundbreaking work of new scholarship, but instead, it builds upon scholarship already done on Ellen G. White's life and ministry. In the past few decades, a new generation of Adventist historians have laid a broad foundation of new research and interpretations that have added depth to Ellen G. White studies. At the same time, such research necessitates fresh attempts at synthesis. This work attempts to make a contribution in this latter category.

We included not only basic terms of reference—such as people, publications, or places—but also specific words, or jargon, familiar to people who lived during Ellen G. White's lifetime. The only previous attempt at this appears in an appendix to volume 3 of the *Comprehensive Index to the Writings of Ellen G. White*, which was created a little over five decades ago. This list included about fifty terms that are helpful. The problem is that this list is brief and represents terms that were unfamiliar practically two generations ago. Many more terms have been added to this original list as the passing of time necessitates additional words or phrases that should be explored. This current list is not intended to be exhaustive. A starting point for this list began by carefully reviewing the nine volumes of *Testimonies for the Church* (1855–1909) and the five volumes of the Conflict of the Ages series (1888–1917). We marked at the back of each volume unusual words or phrases that stood out as unfamiliar. This allowed us to start with our own unique list of words or phrases from her lifetime. A close examination of the words she used, along with grammatical constructions, shows that, like most people, the manner in which she expressed herself changed over time. Although the meaning of words also changed, she sometimes absorbed Victorian rhetoric that historians characterize as direct, uncompromising, and often hyperbolic (Cf. Benjamin McArthur, *A. G. Daniells: Shaper of Twentieth-Century Adventism* [Nampa, ID: Pacific Press®, 2016], 93).

Some theological ideas that were important in Ellen G. White's early life and ministry changed to other priorities during her lifetime. And in other instances, she provided greater clarity and depth to still yet other concepts. Naturally, there were some words or expressions that are only used in a few brief instances. Such brevity, especially when further clarification is limited, necessitates caution with regard to interpretation. In such instances, priority has been given to her own writings when possible to define the meaning of her words. Other tools used include Noah Webster's 1828 dictionary, along with other reference works published during her lifetime. Webster remains especially significant for his sytematization of American grammar and spelling marking the fading away from the earlier colonial British English with movement toward the emerging American English. As already mentioned, not every word or expression could be included in this list; yet this "pocket dictionary" of Ellen G. White attempts to highlight some of the most significant or, at times, most unusual words and phrases. Our goal from the beginning has been to limit the size of this volume to approximately five hundred entries.

The volume has two parts: the first is a general introduction to Ellen G. White and her writings, followed by the second part consisting of the actual entries themselves. Asterisks (*) refer to other pertinent entries; in a few instances, there are cross-references to other entries to avoid unnecessary confusion or duplication.

Finally yet importantly, we are grateful to a number of persons who have helped to make this volume possible. Special thanks are due to Ed Allen, Benjamin Baker, Donny Chrissutianto, Denis Fortin, Anna Galenience, Ronald Graybill, Norman Gulley, Denis Kaiser, Bill Knott, Koberson Langhu, Doug Matacio, Jerry Moon, Eike Mueller, Miguel Patino, Tim Poirier, Nikolaus Satelmajer, Graeme Sharrock, Alberto R. Timm, Cindy Tutsch, Clinton Wahlen, Woodrow W. Whidden II, and Ed Zinke, who at various stages in the journey have offered advice and incisive comments. A debt of gratitude is due to George R. Knight, Brian E. Strayer, and Kevin M. Burton, whose meticulous feedback did much to strengthen the manuscript. Wendy Marcum and Amy Scoggins were invaluable editors who along with Tammie Knauff helped to catch many potential pitfalls. Of course, final responsibility for the content belongs to the authors alone. An additional word of gratitude is due to Jerry D. Thomas, Scott Cady, and Miguel Valdivia, who helped guide this manuscript through the editorial process.

Abbreviations

AA--------------- *The Acts of the Apostles*
AH -------------- *The Adventist Home*
ApM ------------ *An Appeal to Mothers*
1–6BIO --------- *Ellen G. White*, 6 vols.
CCh------------- *Counsels for the Church*
CD -------------- *Counsels on Diet and Foods*
CE--------------- *Christian Education*
CEv ------------- *The Colporteur Evangelist*
CG -------------- *Child Guidance*
CH -------------- *Counsels on Health*
CM-------------- *Colporteur Ministry*
COL ------------ *Christ's Object Lessons*
CS --------------- *Counsels on Stewardship*
CSA ------------- *A Call to Stand Apart*
CT -------------- *Counsels to Parents, Teachers, and Students*
CTBH ---------- *Christian Temperance and Bible Hygiene*
DA -------------- *The Desire of Ages*
Ed --------------- *Education*

1EGWLM ----- *The Ellen G. White Letters and Manuscripts*, vol. 1

Ev --------------- *Evangelism*

EW -------------- *Early Writings of Ellen G. White*

ExV ------------- *A Sketch of the Christian Experience and Views of Ellen G. White*

FE --------------- *Fundamentals of Christian Education*

FLB ------------- *The Faith I Live By*

FW -------------- *Faith and Works*

GC -------------- *The Great Controversy*

GCB ------------ *The General Conference Bulletin*

GW ------------- *Gospel Workers*

HR -------------- *The Health Reformer*

HS -------------- *Historical Sketches of the Foreign Missions of the Seventh-day Adventists*

LS --------------- *Life Sketches of Ellen G. White*

LS80 ------------ *Life Sketches, Ancestry, Early Life, Christian Experience, and Extensive Labors of Elder James White and His Wife, Mrs. Ellen G. White*, 1880 ed.

Lt. --------------- letter

MB -------------- *Thoughts From the Mount of Blessing*

MC -------------- *Manual for Canvassers*

MH ------------- *The Ministry of Healing*

1–21MR ------- *Manuscript Releases*, 21 vols.

1–2MCP ------- *Mind, Character, and Personality*, 2 vols.

Ms --------------- manuscript

OHC ----------- *Our High Calling*

PK --------------- *Prophets and Kings*

PP --------------*Patriarchs and Prophets*
RC -------------*Reflecting Christ*
RH -------------*Review and Herald*
1–2SAT---------*Sermons and Talks*, 2 vols.
SC--------------*Steps to Christ*
1–4SG ---------*Spiritual Gifts*, 4 vols.
SL --------------*The Sanctified Life*
1–3SM ---------*Selected Messages*, 3 vols.
1–4SP----------*Spirit of Prophecy*, 4 vols.
ST --------------*Signs of the Times*
1–9T -----------*Testimonies for the Church*, 9 vols.
TM-------------*Testimonies to Ministers and Gospel Workers*
TSB ------------*Testimonies on Sexual Behavior, Adultery, and Divorce*
YI---------------*The Youth's Instructor*
YRP ------------*Ye Shall Receive Power*

Who Was Ellen G. White?

Ellen G. White was an exceptional person. As an American prophet, she received hundreds of dreams and visions that she credited as revelations from God. Her literary output—approximately one hundred thousand pages—is nothing short of staggering. Several of her most important works, *Steps to Christ*, *The Desire of Ages*, and *The Great Controversy*, are classics in their own right. Each have had multiple editions, were translated in numerous languages, and remain in print to this day. Tens of millions of copies of her works have been distributed around the world. The appeal of her thought continues through articles, reviews, dissertations, and conferences, despite the fact that she never saw herself as an academic. Instead, she gave practical advice through "testimonies" for those near and far. She cofounded the Seventh-day Adventist Church with her husband, James, and Joseph Bates. After they passed away, she lived for more than three decades as a pivotal influence upon the formation and development of the denomination. Her writings continue to challenge and inspire lay readers as well as scholars.

Although her pen has had a lasting influence, her life

involved far more. She was an activist in a host of religious and social reforms. Ellen Gould Harmon and her twin, Elizabeth, were born on November 26, 1827, near Gorham, Maine, to Robert and Eunice Harmon. Like many evangelicals of her time, she experienced a dramatic conversion after a near-death experience. Several years later she gave her heart to Jesus Christ and applied for baptism in the Chestnut Street Methodist church. Pastor John Hobart baptized her in Casco Bay, Portland, Maine, on June 26, 1842. That same year Ellen heard the revivalist William Miller preach about the soon return of Jesus Christ. She later described this time as the "happiest year" of her life (LS80 187).

After the Great Disappointment, when Christ did not return as the "little flock" expected on October 22, 1844, she became discouraged (LS80 189). It was also around this time that physicians diagnosed her with tuberculosis. The chronic illness was so debilitating that her mother, Eunice, had to stay up all night to prevent Ellen from choking on her own blood. Another Millerite friend, Elizabeth Haines, offered to take care of her; this is how Ellen happened to be at her home with a group of women on an unknown morning in December 1844 when she received her first vision. Together, as they knelt in prayer, she was shown a scattered group of Advent believers on a pathway from this world to heaven. At the beginning of the path was a light, which she was told was the "midnight cry" message about the near advent of Christ (EW 14). At the other end of the path was a much brighter light where she saw Jesus. So long as the pilgrims on the pathway kept their eyes on Jesus, they were safe; but some took their eyes off Him and fell into the darkness below. The vision served as a confirmation that the Advent believers' experience was not in vain. Although initially hesitant, Ellen gained courage and began to share her visionary experiences in public. At first, she traveled with family members, but later she was also accompanied by another Millerite lecturer, James White. The two were wed on August 30, 1846.

During the next few years, they wrestled over the cause of their disappointment. From Joseph Bates, they learned about the seventh-day *Sabbath, although they feared initially "that Bro. B. erred in dwelling upon the fourth commandment more than the other nine" (2SG 82). Later, after studying the issue further, they conceded that Bates was right and also accepted the new interpretation of the sanctuary as advocated by O. R. L. Crosier, Hiram Edson, and others in western New York. They believed that Miller had mistaken this earth as the sanctuary that was to be cleansed in Daniel 8:14; instead there was a cleansing of the sanctuary in heaven as Christ moved from the Holy Place to the Most Holy Place, which must take place before the Second Coming. This "investigative judgment" gradually changed their missiological perspective.

From 1848 to 1850, James and Ellen G. White, along with Joseph Bates, participated in a series of conferences across the northeastern United States. They shared their views with other disappointed Millerites. Slowly, a body of believers coalesced that rallied around two new serial publications: the *Present Truth* and the *Advent Review*. After 1850, they merged into the *Second Advent Review and Sabbath Herald*. Although small at first, Ellen G. White predicted that it would grow to become "like streams of light that went clear round the world" (LS 125).

The Whites relocated several times during this early period, settling in Rochester, New York, from 1851 to 1855. They continued to struggle financially. The Whites responded to an offer from believers to build them a publishing house and home in Battle Creek, Michigan, in 1855. The denomination formally organized there in 1863, and Battle Creek remained the center of the Adventist work until a series of disasters struck in 1902. This subsequently led to the transition of the church headquarters to Takoma Park, Maryland.

During these early years, Ellen G. White became a mother to four boys: Henry Nichols (1847–1863), James Edson (1849–1928), William Clarence (1854–1937), and John Herbert (1860). One of the most difficult struggles of her life, she stated, was to leave her children behind in the care of others as she maintained a vigorous travel schedule (LS 165). She wrote frequent letters to her children; and as they grew older, they increasingly traveled with their parents. Tragically, young John Herbert died from *erysipelas, a skin infection, when he was less than three months old. "At times I could not control my feelings as I witnessed his sufferings," she exclaimed. "But our heavenly Father saw fit to remove my lovely babe" (2SG 296). Later Henry died while spending the summer with close family friends in Maine. In her later years, Ellen G. White, as a health reformer, regretted that she did not know more about health reform during this early stage in their lives. Of the two remaining children, Edson was more of a rebel, who caused them grief. He left the church for a short period only to experience a conversion later on in life and served successfully as a missionary to black Americans in the southern United States. Ellen's precious "Willie" was always the son who took care of his mother after his father's death in 1881.

The Seventh-day Adventist Church grew significantly, particularly during the late 1850s through the 1860s, when many organizational developments took place. The name *Seventh-day Adventist* was chosen in 1860; and the following year the publishing house was incorporated, along with the earliest conference. By 1863, the Seventh-day Adventist Church was officially organized under the auspices of a General Conference. On June 5, 1863, soon after the church's organization, Ellen G. White received a far-reaching health-reform vison. From this vision, she described the importance of the whole body and the need to pay attention to natural laws and to use natural remedies, in contrast to the many poisonous drugs that were typically prescribed at that time. By 1872, the Seventh-day Adventist General Conference acquired the "Select School" that had formed in Battle Creek, Michigan, with *Goodloe Harper Bell as the first teacher. That school quickly expanded to become the *Battle Creek College two years later. The year 1874 witnessed the departure of the first American-born denominationally sponsored missionaries: John Nevins Andrews, with his children Mary and Charles, expanded the Adventist presence on the European continent. Adventist education and missions would expand significantly in subsequent decades.

Ellen G. White's personal life, as well as the denomination, suffered a significant setback with the death of James White; after a series of debilitating strokes and malaria, he finally succumbed to malaria in 1881. Afterward, her son Willie White would frequently travel with her and support his mother's ministry and writing work. From 1885 to 1887, they traveled through Europe, helping organize and support the missionary work, including resolving conflicts between missionaries. Ellen articulated a missiological principle of developing missionary centers, resolutely urged the continued expansion of Adventist missions, and set the example herself when she went to Australia from 1891 to 1900.

The final years of Ellen G. White, from the time she returned from Australia until her death on July 16, 1915, at Elmshaven, near St. Helena, California, were characterized by a surge in productivity in terms of her writing. She, assisted as she was by a staff of secretaries and editors, continued to counsel church leaders and was active in the reorganization of the General Conference in 1901. She also supported A. G. Daniells, a young minister and missionary, who had experience (with Willie White) in developing union conferences (groups of conferences) and restructuring the denomination.

Ellen G. White and the Bible

Fundamental to understanding Ellen G. White is her view of the Bible. Almost every page of her extensive published writings contains a scriptural quotation, reference, or allusion. The Bible is, without a doubt, central to all her writings. After recounting her early visions in her first book, *A Sketch of the Christian Experience and Views of Ellen G. White*, she said of the Bible: "I recommend to you, dear reader, the word of God as the rule of your faith and practice. By that Word we are to be judged. God has, in that Word, promised to give visions in the 'last days;' not for a new rule of faith, but for the comfort of his people, and to correct those who err from Bible truth" (64). This statement is significant because it reveals how she understood her visions in relationship to the Bible early in her prophetic ministry. The Bible, she said, was the final rule for "faith and practice," and the visions were never to take the place of the Bible.

Sixty years later, after more visions and study of Scripture, this position had only matured. In the 1911 edition of *The Great Controversy*, she affirmed her lifelong position on the final authority of the Bible in relationship to the work of the Spirit in her prophetic ministry:

> In His word, God has committed to men the knowledge necessary for salvation. The Holy Scriptures are to be accepted as an authoritative, infallible revelation of His will. They are the standard of character, the revealer of doctrines, and the test of experience. . . .
>
> The Spirit was not given—nor can it ever be bestowed—to supersede the Bible; for the Scriptures explicitly state that the word of God is the standard by which all teaching and experience must be tested (vii).

Over the years, she repeatedly set forth her writings as subject to the Bible, rather than as an addition to it: "The Lord desires you to study your Bibles. He has not given any additional light to take the place of his Word. This light is to bring confused minds to his Word, which, if eaten and digested, is as the lifeblood of the soul" (3SM 29). In 1901, she urged the General Conference leaders to uphold the Bible as their primary authority: "Lay Sister White to one side. Do not quote my words again as long as you live until you can obey the Bible. When you make the Bible your food, your meat and your drink, when you make its principles the elements of your character, you will know better how to receive counsel from God. I exalt the precious Word before you today. Do not repeat what I have said, saying, 'Sister White said this,' and 'Sister White said that.' Find out what the Lord God of Israel says, and then do what He commands" (13MR 200).

With compelling power, she stressed the importance of the Bible as the place for Christians to hear the voice of God: "The Bible is God's voice speaking to us, just as surely as though we could hear it with our ears. If we realized this, with what awe would we open God's word, and with what earnestness would we search its precepts! The reading and contemplation of the Scriptures would be regarded as an audience with the Infinite One" (6T 393).

Ellen G. White's most memorable analogy of the relationship of her writings to the Bible occurs in the following statement: "Little heed is given to the Bible, and the Lord has given a lesser light to lead men and women to the greater light" (3SM 30). This greater-light, lesser-light comparison suggests that just as the moon derives its light from the sun and only reflects the emittance from that source, so her messages derive their authority from Scripture, reflect its teaching, and lead others to it as the basis for Christian living and doctrine. Thus, if students of Ellen G. White heed her, they will study the Bible first to understand God's will and then go to her writings.

How to Interpret Ellen G. White's Writings

At the time of her death in 1915, Ellen G. White had produced more than one hundred thousand pages of published material. With such a large body of writings, written during an era (1845–1915) far removed from our twenty-first-century world, correct principles of interpretation are essential to understand her message. The following eight guidelines will aid the student in understanding the intended meaning of Ellen G. White's writings:

1. Study the Bible first, then go to Ellen G. White's writings. Ellen G. White never meant for her writings to be read in place of the Bible. For her, Scripture was the supreme source of God's revelation (*see* Bible; revelation and inspiration; and authority). "God's Word is the unerring standard. The Testimonies are not to take the place of the Word," she declared (Ev 256). Throughout her seventy-year prophetic ministry, her attitude toward the Bible was expressed thus: "My brethren and sisters, go to the Bible, and from it learn God's will concerning you" (5MR 250). Regular readers of

Ellen G. White's writings should make their first priority the study of the Bible.

Because Ellen G. White's writings are a manifestation of the postbiblical prophetic gift, the function of her writings is to give an inspired application of the Bible. Just as the biblical prophet Huldah authoritatively applied Scripture to her audience (2 Chronicles 34:24–28), so Ellen G. White applied Scripture in her writings. Thus, it only makes sense for readers of Ellen G. White to go first to the source from which the application comes. In this way, her writings are better understood and appreciated.

The order of reading should, therefore, be the following:

Bible → Ellen G. White

It should *not* be as follows:

Ellen G. White → Bible

2. Study all available information on a given topic. When studying a topic in Ellen G. White's writings, such as the Holy Spirit, the 144,000, or prayer, one should listen to the wide spectrum of her counsel. An isolated statement here or there does not always give the complete picture of her teaching on a subject. The Ellen G. White Estate has a text searchable website that includes virtually all of her published and unpublished writings (https://egwwritings.org). Its search engine enables the student to instantly pull up every instance in which a term or phrase is used in all her published writings. Reading through these references provides a more comprehensive understanding of Ellen G. White's thoughts on a topic. But a word of caution is in order: if the statements are not read in their literary context, the tendency is to read one's own ideas into them. The next hermeneutical guideline is a good antidote for this dangerous practice.

3. Study each statement in its immediate and larger literary context. In Ellen G. White's writings, the literary context is the paragraphs, pages, documents, and books surrounding a particular statement. In the case of a letter, manuscript, or published article, one must look at a sentence or paragraph in light of the surrounding paragraphs and then as part of the entire document. In the case of a book, one must view the statement noting the surrounding paragraphs and pages in a chapter and eventually in light of the entire book. Regarding the larger context, every statement should be viewed in light of the Conflict of the Ages series. These five volumes—*Patriarchs and Prophets*, *Prophets and Kings*, *The Desire of Ages*, *The Acts of the Apostles*, and *The Great Controversy*—provide the theological framework for Ellen G. White's writings. They reflect her most mature theological thought on themes appearing earlier in her writings and thus should be carefully understood by any interpreter.

The practice of using a statement from Ellen G. White out of its context disrupts the flow of her thought. Like any organized writer, her flow of thought was a series of related ideas that she carefully laid out to communicate a specific concept. This meaningful communication involved a type of logical thought progression in which one thought led naturally to the next. In this way, she communicated like most people communicate—with a series of selected ideas, all linked together in a logical pattern. Thus, each sentence she wrote must be understood in light of the other ideas expressed in the context, which is her train of thought. To insert a foreign meaning, contrary to her original intention, is a violation of her rights as an author. Yet this is what some readers do with her writings on a regular basis.

Ellen G. White was very aware of the issue of literary

context in her writings. On several occasions, she commented on the way her writings were taken out of context:

> Many men take the testimonies the Lord has given, and apply them as they suppose they should be applied, picking out a sentence here and there, taking it from its proper connection, and applying it according to their idea. Thus poor souls become bewildered, when could they read in order all that has been given, they would see the true application, and would not become confused. Much that purports to be a message from Sister White, serves the purpose of misrepresenting Sister White, making her testify in favor of things that are not in accordance with her mind or judgment (1SM 44).

In the same vein, she wrote, "Those who are not walking in the light of the message may gather up statements from my writings that happen to please them, and that agree with their human judgment, and, by separating these statements from their connection, and placing them beside human reasonings, make it appear that my writings uphold that which they condemn" (Lt. 208, 1906). In both of these statements, she uses the word *connection*; this carries the same meaning as the word *context*. Ellen G. White was thus sensitive to the way her writings were taken out of context by her followers. At one point of frustration, she remarked,

> What I might say in private conversations would be so repeated as to make it mean exactly opposite to what it would have meant had the hearers been sanctified in mind and spirit. I am afraid to speak even to my friends; for afterwards I hear, Sister White said this, or Sister White said that.

> My words are so wrested and misinterpreted that I am coming to the conclusion that the Lord desires me to keep out of large assemblies and refuse private interviews (3SM 82).

4. Study each statement in its historical context. Ellen G. White lived most of her life during the latter half of the nineteenth century. This general historical period, with its rapidly changing religious, political, and cultural landscape was the historical context of her day-to-day life experience. She lived through such political events as the war with Mexico (1846–1848), the Civil War (1861–1865), Reconstruction after the Civil War (1865–1877), the Spanish-American War (1898), and the beginning of World War I (1914–1918). Other important contexts include the foreign missionary movement (1810–early 1900s), the urbanization of America (1870s–1920s), and the temperance movement (1870s–1930s). She also observed and experienced the growth of spiritualism, the expansion of evangelicalism, the initiation of numerous social reforms, and the perpetuation of racial tensions. This rich and varied background cannot be ignored in the interpretation of her writings any more than the historical context of first-century Palestine can be ignored in interpreting the teachings of Jesus.

In the more specific historical context of the Seventh-day Adventist Church, time, place, and circumstances are the keys to unlocking the meaning of many of Ellen G. White's statements penned over a seventy-year period. On more than one occasion, she specified the importance of these categories for interpreting her writings. Regarding time, she wrote in 1875, concerning the advancement of the work of God, "that which may be said in truth of individuals at one time may not correctly be said of them at another time" (3T 471). Concerning circumstances in her writings, she stated in 1904 that "circumstances alter conditions. Circumstances change the relation of things" (3SM 217). Referring to her writings in 1911, she penned, "Regarding the testimonies, nothing is ignored; nothing is cast aside; but time and place must be considered" (1SM 57). Thus, Ellen G. White expressed concern that her readers keep the historical context of her writings in mind.

Several resources for understanding the historical context of Ellen G. White's writings are Arthur L. White's six-volume biography *Ellen G. White*; George R. Knight's *Ellen White's World: A Fascinating Look at the Times in Which She Lived*; Jud Lake's *A Nation in God's Hands*; *The World of Ellen G. White*, edited by Gary Land; and *The Ellen G. White Encyclopedia*, edited by Denis Fortin and Jerry Moon.

5. Discover the underlying principles. In the study of Ellen G. White's writings, it is important to understand the difference between principles and applications. A *principle* is a universal, timeless rule of human conduct or behavior. An *application* is when a principle is used in a specific, historically conditioned situation. For example, Mrs. White counseled men to "let their beards remain unshaven, . . . until the Sabbath is past" (ST May 25, 1882). Some take this statement as Sabbath keeping legislation that present-day Adventists do not follow. What Seventh-day Adventist preacher today, they argue, would come to church unshaven?

This is a classic case of overlooking the historical setting of the statement. In 1882, when this statement was penned, shaving consumed much more time than it does today. Men had to mix their own soap lather and sharpen their handheld straight razors on leather bands called *strops*. Today, because of electric shavers, shaving is a simple process, taking only a few minutes at most. Ellen G. White's application of the underlying principle—avoiding any unnecessary labor that interferes with the spirit of the Sabbath—fit the historical context of shaving in the nineteenth century. Would she tell men not to shave today? No. Most twenty-first-century Adventist men, depending on their culture, do not view shaving as violating the spirit of the Sabbath. But the underlying principle remains normative and can be applied to other activities. Therefore always look for the underlying, timeless principles.

6. Stay balanced, and avoid extreme interpretations. Adventist history is replete with people who had extreme interpretations of Ellen G. White's writings. Although balance typified her writings, this has not always been found in her followers. Some, for example, have taken her counsel "eggs should not be placed upon your table" (2T 399) to mean that all Seventh-day Adventists should not eat eggs. These readers have, however, missed the historical context of this letter in which Mrs. White addressed a specific family struggling with their diet (2T 712). She never meant this counsel to be applied to all Seventh-day Adventists, and she provided a balancing statement: "While warnings have been given regarding the dangers of disease through butter, and the evil of the free use of eggs by small children, yet we should not consider it a violation of principle to use eggs from hens that are well cared for and suitably fed. Eggs contain properties that are remedial agencies in counteracting certain poisons" (CD 207). The historical context of these statements reveals the balanced approach Ellen White took with regard to dietary counsel. Frustrated with those who had taken "extreme views of health reform" after reading her writings, she wrote that "health reform becomes *health deform*, a health destroyer, when it is carried to extremes" (CD 202; emphasis added). Thus, one should always look for balancing statements in Ellen G. White's writings.

Concerning those who would take radical views of her writings, she wrote:

> It is the desire and plan of Satan to bring in among us those who will go to great extremes—people of narrow minds, who are critical and sharp, and very tenacious in holding their own conceptions of what the truth means. They will be exacting, and will seek to enforce rigorous duties, and go to great lengths in matters of minor importance, while they neglect the weightier matters of the law—judgment and mercy and the love of God. Through the work of a few of this class of persons, the whole body of Sabbath-keepers will be designated as bigoted, Pharisaical, and fanatical. The work of the truth, because of these workers, will be thought to be unworthy of notice (Ev 212).

7. Remember that inspiration is not verbal dictation. Although Ellen G. White took a more whole-person view of inspiration, some of her followers have taken a more rigid view known as *verbal dictation.* This view maintains that every word was dictated to the prophet by God. A classic example of this view of inspiration is found in the understanding of Dr. David Paulson, a cofounder of Hinsdale Sanitarium, who wrote to Ellen G. White and stated: "I was led to conclude and most firmly believe that *every* word that you ever spoke in public or private, that every letter you wrote under *any* and *all* circumstances, was as inspired as the Ten Commandments" (emphasis in the original). Her response was direct: "My brother," she penned, "you have studied my writings diligently, and you have never found that I have made any such claims, neither will you find that the pioneers in our cause ever made such claims." In the rest of her letter, she reinforced this statement with citations from her earlier writings on the topic (1SM 24).

Inspiration and interpretation go together like hand in

glove. Those supporters of Ellen G. White who espouse a more rigid view of inspiration tend to place too much emphasis on her words and sentences, void of their literary context, and consequently develop legalistic interpretations and applications. Detractors with a rigid view of inspiration also tend to emphasize words and sentences over context but use this view as a weapon to discredit Ellen G. White's teaching. Neither of these approaches to inspiration and interpretation is biblical or correct (see Jud Lake, *Ellen White Under Fire*, chap. 6).

8. Maintain a healthy, spiritual mind-set. In *Reading Ellen White* (Hagerstown, MD: Review and Herald®, 1997), George R. Knight suggests two guidelines for maintaining a healthy, spiritual mind-set while reading Ellen G. White:

> First, begin your study with a prayer for guidance and understanding. The Holy Spirit, who inspired the work of prophets across the ages, is the only one who is in a position to unlock the meaning in their writings. . . .
>
> Second, we need to approach our study with an open mind. Most of us realize that no person is free of bias, no one is completely open-minded. We also recognize that bias enters into every area of our lives. But that reality doesn't mean that we need to let our biases control us (43).

A vital component of reading Ellen G. White's writings is to remember that they are not an "iron rod" to be used against others. Instead, it is vital to read them for oneself and live out those counsels consistently by applying them to one's own life. In this way, as Christian believers, we should show a spirit of love and tolerance toward others who may be at other points in their spiritual growth.

Another essential aspect is to maintain faith and trust in God, to exercise faith and avoid doubt. Concerning doubt, Ellen G. White counseled, "Many think it a virtue, a mark of intelligence in them, to be unbelieving and to question and quibble. Those who desire to doubt will have plenty of room. God does not propose to remove all occasion for unbelief. He gives evidence, which must be carefully investigated with a humble mind and a teachable spirit, and all should decide from the weight of evidence" (3T 255).

As you begin or expand your journey into Ellen G. White's writings, it is our hope that you will read them for yourself. As you do so, we hope the following entries will be helpful.

Entries

A

abstemious/abstemiousness. A term used by Ellen G. White to emphasize a temperate lifestyle that avoids anything harmful to the body. From her perspective, John the Baptist was a model of an abstemious life (DA 100, 101, 275). She frequently recommended an "abstemious diet" as a key to healthful living (4T 501).

Adventist. A term used to describe a believer in the *second coming of Jesus Christ; most often used as a shortened form for Seventh-day Adventist after the organization of the denomination in 1863. Also used to refer to the followers of *William Miller.

Advent Review. A publication from 1850 that was combined with the *Present Truth* in 1850 to form the *Second Advent Review and Sabbath Herald*, which later became the *Review and Herald*, and today is known as the *Adventist Review* and *Adventist World*.

affable. Easy to get along with. Ellen G. White describes "affable" as an important characteristic for husbands and fathers (2T 383) and that Adventist youth should look to the affable example of the biblical Daniel (YI May 10, 1900).

affection(s). A term to describe human emotion(s) in regard to one another and to God. "True affection will overlook many mistakes; love will not discern them" (AH 47).

air. Ellen G. White highlighted the importance of pure and fresh air as being essential for health. The lungs need "full inspiration" lest the blood not be "properly vitalized" (MH 292). The word "air" can be used in a phrase such as "an air of piety" (DA 256) or "an air of authority" (DA 133) to describe certain situations.

alacrity. Cheerful and quick response to action. She admonished young mothers, for example, "to perform with alacrity the plain, uninteresting, homely, but most needful duties which relate to domestic life" (CG 74). Church workers should "labor with earnest alacrity" so that everything done "will bear the signature of God, and will make its impression on human minds" (GCB June 3, 1909).

Albigenses. Inhabitants of southern France who resisted Roman Catholic control. Ellen G. White portrayed them as the brethren of the *Waldenses (GC 271). *See also* Waldensians.

almoners. People who collect alms for the poor (9T 53).

amalgamation. A controversial term used in antebellum America (before the American Civil War) in a pejorative sense to describe the intermingling of races. Ellen G. White used the term to describe how Satan corrupted the world (3SG 64, 75; 1SP 69, 78). She also used the term in a moral sense to denote the combination of good with evil, which corrupts the good. This term is used by critics to allege that Ellen G. White was a racist; but the overall thrust of her life, both before and after the Civil War, indicates that she was an ardent abolitionist and committed to race equality.

American Sentinel. A Seventh-day Adventist publication printed from 1886 to 1900 that advocated religious liberty. It was replaced in 1900 by the *Sentinel of Liberty*. In December 1901, it changed its name to *The Sentinel of Christian Liberty*, and continued until February 11, 1904, when it vanished until it was reborn with the shortened name of *Liberty* in 1906.

Andrews, John Nevins (1829–1883). Minister, author, and close friend of James and Ellen G. White. Converted in 1843, he began to observe the seventh-day *Sabbath in 1845. He first met the Whites in 1849 during which time Ellen G. White rebuked the rampant fanaticism of some Adventists. Andrews began pastoral ministry in 1850 and in 1856 married Angeline Stevens (1824–1872). For a time, Andrews gave up the ministry to farm in Waukon, Iowa, but returned to ministry in 1859. It was while he was there that he wrote the first edition of his seminal work *History of the Sabbath and First Day of the Week* (1859). Ellen G. White reproved the Andrews family several times, which prompted confessions. Andrews is the "Brother A" in volume 3 of *Testimonies for the Church* (14, 15). In 1874, Andrews, along with his two children, Mary and Charles, went with Adhemar Vuilleumier, a student from Switzerland who had completed some training at Battle Creek, as the first official American-born denominationally sponsored missionaries of the Seventh-day Adventist Church. Mary tragically died from tuberculosis in 1878. Ellen G. White's severest rebuke to Andrews came in 1883, which prompted another contrite letter of *repentance. Andrews also succumbed to tuberculosis on October 21, 1883.

angels. Supernatural beings that play a significant role in the *great controversy between Christ and Satan. According to Ellen White, heavenly angels are "ministering spirits" under the command of Christ "sent forth to minister for them who shall be heirs of salvation" (Hebrews 1:14). Fallen angels are the "principalities and powers" under the command of Satan who fight against God's government (Ephesians 6:12). Ellen White was very cognizant about the nearness of angels. She described "holy angels" who protect the followers of Christ. Such a recognition should be a "truth most comfortable and precious to every follower of Christ," as evidenced in Scripture (GC 551). Angels appeared in the Garden of Eden where they often visited to give "counsel and instruction" (Ed 21). Angels can appear in human form and can even intervene in human politics (GC 631, 632; Ed 305). She described how at certain pivotal moments in salvation history angels specifically protected God's people and how they watch with special interest the unfolding of the plan of salvation (Ed 126). Angels watched over and ministered to Jesus Christ while He was on Earth (ST Dec. 9, 1897). She also described "angels of God" who watched over *Martin Luther at the Diet of Worms (GC 150). Each person has a guardian angel (Ed 305). It is the office of heavenly angels to prepare the heart to comprehend God's Word (GC 600). They are furthermore "ministers and witnesses" during the investigative judgment (GC 479). They comfort God's people during times of trouble and record every "earnest and sincere" *prayer (GC 621, 622). Could human beings only see with "heavenly vision, they would behold companies of angels" (GC 630). Human beings are coworkers with angels in the *work of redemption here on Earth (Ed 271). Ellen White's most significant statement on evil angels reads thus: "The power and malice of Satan and his host might justly alarm us were it not that we may find shelter and deliverance in the superior power of our Redeemer. We carefully secure our houses with bolts and locks to protect our property and our lives from evil men; but we seldom think of the evil angels who are constantly seeking access to us, and against whose attacks we have, in our own strength, no method of defense. If permitted, they can distract our minds, disorder and torment our bodies, destroy our possessions and our lives. Their only delight is in misery and destruction. Fearful is the condition of those who resist the divine claims and yield to Satan's temptations, until God gives them up to the control of evil spirits. But those who follow Christ are ever safe under His watchcare. Angels that excel in strength are sent from heaven to protect them. The wicked one cannot break through the guard which God has stationed about His people" (GC 518).

animal magnetism. The belief that the bodies of animals and humans contained a magnetic fluid that allowed for those with a large amount of this fluid in their system to be put into a deep sleep or trance. Experimentation with this theory became very popular and found its greatest advocate in Franz Anton Mesmer, who practiced in Paris and used his theory to heal people of their ailments. His theories, known as *mesmerism, were extremely popular during the nineteenth century and developed into what is now known as *hypnosis*.

animal passions/propensities. A common *Victorian term used to refer to the inner emotions, especially as they related to sex and sexuality. The term was popularized by Orson Fowler, Lydia Folger Fowler, and Lorenzo Fowler, who promoted *phrenology, to describe social instincts of *adhesiveness* (friendship) and *amativeness* (love between the sexes), which were thought to occupy a large section of the brain with a tremendous power for good or ill. When either the adhesiveness or amativeness became overactive, the results could be disastrous. Ellen G. White described stimulating food that caused an unnatural excitement and therefore aroused the animal passions (4T 140, 141). Christians should avoid being "dragged down to a level with the brutes" (PP 458).

anti-Trinitarian. *See* Godhead.

apoplexy. A term that stems from the ancient Greek ἀποπληξία (*apoplēxia*), meaning "a striking away." In the nineteenth century, it was a vague term that implied some kind of mental impairment, such as a stroke (CD 386; 1T 520).

apples of gold. A biblical phrase used to describe something that becomes beautiful and good. Sometimes used in the full phrase "apples of gold in pictures of silver" (Proverbs 25:11).

approbation. A term that points to the approval or praise of other human beings (5T 222) or of God (5T 113). A grave danger that human beings should avoid is developing a "love of approbation" (PP 650).

artificials. Hairpiece or hat. Often used in conjunction with tight pins and a wrap that made the head hot; a condition that Ellen G. White protested against (3T 376).

associates. A term used to describe friends.

assurance of salvation. Ellen G. White believed that the biblical assurance of salvation is essential to normal Christian experience (1SM 373; 2SM 255). She urged moderation regarding the extreme of those who become self-confident and prideful of their salvation. Such persons must be vigilant lest they become spiritually blind and boast of their own strength instead of trusting in Jesus. Another extreme that she viewed with caution involved those who were afraid to trust and have confidence in the ability of Jesus Christ to save them. Such a person "worries himself out of the arms of Jesus" (2T 98). She advocated for "Christian zeal" that is "controlled by principle." Believers should have *faith and confidence in God's ability to save them, even though they may not necessarily feel that they are worthy to be saved. For those who have difficulty in the Christian life, the problem is not the ability of Christ to save, but a divided heart. She consistently pointed people to surrender their hearts to Jesus Christ as the basis for the assurance of salvation (2T 232–235).

atonement. The atonement of Jesus Christ on the cross of Calvary is a central and overarching theme in Ellen G. White's writings. Theologians generally view the atonement through a variety of categories including the objective, subjective, and moral government theories. White extrapolated from all of these theories as she saw the atonement as something complex that extends beyond finite human knowledge. In strict theological terms, her views coincide most closely with the *moral government of God. "Henceforth Christ's followers are to look upon Satan as a conquered foe. Upon the cross, Jesus was to gain the victory for them; that victory He desired them to accept as their own" (MH 94).

attachment. A *Victorian term to indicate a relationship; the modern equivalent of being in a relationship. Ellen G. White describes how Saul's daughter Michal fell in love or developed an "attachment" for David (PP 652).

authority. Ellen G. White believed that the *Bible, as revealed in the Old and New Testaments, was the very Word of God (5T 235) and the highest authority for the Christian. "The Holy Scriptures," she declared, "are to be accepted as an authoritative, infallible revelation of His will. They are the standard of character, the revealer of doctrines, and the test of experience"

(GC vii). She also believed that the *Holy Spirit is not only "the author of the Scriptures" but also the author of the "Spirit of Prophecy [a reference to her writings]" (2MR 189). This statement reflects her view that *inspiration has no degrees and is full and complete in all true prophets. But there are degrees of authority. The postbiblical prophetic gift can never equal or supersede the Bible because its authority is derived from the Bible. Ellen G. White thus described her writings as a "lesser light to lead men and women to the greater light [the Bible]" (CM 125). In her first book of visions, *A Sketch of the Christian Experience and Views of Ellen G. White*, she concluded with a significant nod to the Bible as the supreme source of authority, thus setting the tone that would resonate throughout her writings for more than sixty years: "I recommend to you, dear reader, the word of God as the rule of your faith and practice. By that Word we are to be judged. God has, in that Word, promised to give visions in the 'last days;' not for a new rule of faith, but for the comfort of his people, and to correct those who err from Bible truth" (64).

automaton. A term used to describe a person without the power of free will or choice (PP 49, 331).

avarice/avaricious. To be selfish and eager to benefit oneself, especially with regard to money. "God has been displeased," wrote Ellen G. White, "with Sabbathkeepers for their avaricious spirit" (1T 535). She noted that Christians should control the desire of avarice and for power (PP 440). Similarly, some of the Jews during Jesus' time hardened their hearts due to avarice (DA 156, 157). "The love of money was the ruling passion in the Jewish age. Worldliness usurped the place of God and religion in the soul. So it is now. Avaricious greed for wealth exerts such a fascinating, bewitching influence" (MB 88, 89).

Avondale Health Retreat. A small medical institution located in Cooranbong, New South Wales, Australia, on a portion of the *Avondale School property. The institution, built in 1899, lasted only a short time.

Avondale School. A term used to describe the educational institution in Cooranbong, New South Wales, Australia. Property was purchased in 1894, and the school opened in 1897. Today the school is known as Avondale College of Higher Education.

B

baleful. Threatening harm or menace. Ellen G. White used the word most often in the expression "baleful influence" to describe a variety of threats to the Christian life. For example, she describes "doubt and unbelief" that exercise "their baleful influence over mind and heart" (PK 170).

Ballenger, Albion Fox (1861–1921). Seventh-day Adventist minister known for his advocacy of religious liberty. In 1894, he became an associate editor of the **American Sentinel.* He is best known for his 1897 sermon "Receive Ye the Holy Ghost" that ushered in a strong holiness version of Adventism. By 1905, he questioned the *sanctuary *doctrine; this led to his ultimate dismissal from the denomination. Ellen G. White strongly warned against his views. He later wrote *Cast Out for the Cross of Christ* (1909) about his journey out of Adventism and published the *Gathering Call*, a dissident magazine.

Bangs, Elizabeth (Harmon) (1827–1891). Twin sister of Ellen G. White. She never became a Sabbath keeper, but the two sisters enjoyed a close relationship.

baptism. A sacred ordinance of Christian initiation through full immersion of the recipient in water to symbolize outwardly the inward *conversion of the heart. In line with the *Protestant Reformation, Ellen G. White rejected the Roman Catholic practice of baptism as an exorcism and anointing as a divine rite, but instead, agreed with the Anabaptist rejection of sprinkling as well as infant baptism. A person should be accountable before God to make their own individual choice through baptism.

Barr, Eri L. (1814–1864). First black Seventh-day Adventist minister. Originally a Millerite, in 1852 he accepted the seventh-day Sabbath. Later that year Ellen G. White was shown in vision that Barr was among those preachers "to be depended upon" (1EGWLM 788).

Bates, Joseph (1792–1872). Sea captain, minister, *temperance advocate, and reformer. Bates was one of the cofounders of the Seventh-day Adventist Church and the theological architect of Sabbatarian Adventist theology during the 1840s and 1850s. After his retirement from seafaring, he became a Christian Connexion layperson and was involved in a host of reforms, including abolitionism and the burgeoning temperance movement. He later became active during the *Millerite revival and waited for Christ to come on October 22, 1844. Like others, Bates was severely disappointed when Christ did not return. By the spring of 1845, he read *T. M. Preble's pamphlet and accepted the seventh day as the *Sabbath. He wrote the 1846 tract *The Seventh Day Sabbath, a Perpetual Sign* (revised in 1847). He later adopted the *sanctuary *doctrine from *Hiram Edson and integrated Sabbatarian Adventist theology around the *great controversy theme. Bates was a strong supporter of Ellen G. White's prophetic ministry and contributed to the publication *A Word to the "Little Flock"* (1847).

bath. A method of soaking the body or cleansing it in water. In an age in which baths were infrequent, Ellen White encouraged regular baths. She also understood the word *bath* as a treatment room for hydrotherapy. *Hydrotherapy* is the use of water, particularly through alternating hot and cold treatments, for the cure of disease.

Battle Creek Church. Battle Creek is a town in south-central Michigan that from 1855 to 1903 housed the headquarters of the Seventh-day Adventist Church, including major church institutions such as the *Battle Creek Sanitarium, *Battle Creek College, and the Review and Herald Publishing Association. Ellen G. White wrote more *testimonies to the church in Battle Creek than to any other congregation during her lifetime. "Our people in Battle Creek have greater responsibilities to bear than those in any other place," she noted (4T 518).

Battle Creek College. The school was founded in 1874 as the first permanent Seventh-day Adventist educational institution. It operated in Battle Creek, Michigan, until 1901 when it was relocated to Berrien Springs, Michigan, and renamed Emmanuel Missionary College. In 1960, the institution was renamed Andrews University.

Battle Creek Sanitarium. Founded in 1866 as the Western *Health Reform Institute, it was renamed in 1877 by Dr. *J. H. Kellogg as the Battle Creek Medical and Surgical Sanitarium. During its heyday (by 1900), it was the largest medical institution of its kind in the world. Ellen G. White issued a series of strong admonitions, warning about the spiritual condition of church leaders in Battle Creek, Michigan. Tragically, the institution burned to the ground in 1902. Despite warnings from Ellen G. White to disperse resources, Dr. J. H. Kellogg rebuilt the institution to be even larger than before, which drove a wedge between him and denominational leaders. By 1906, he took the Battle Creek Sanitarium out of denominational ownership, which resulted in his being disfellowshiped from the denomination.

bazaar. Selling goods as a fund-raiser. Ellen G. White warns against careless raising of money in churches, particularly if the place for God's worship is desecrated (COL 54).

Belden, Franklin Edson (1858–1945). Talented musician and son of Ellen G. White's sister Sarah. At the age of thirty, he worked for the Review and Herald Publishing Association but subsequently left the denomination after a series of lawsuits. He later went on to compose songs for Billy Sunday. In his later life, he became one of Ellen G. White's most bitter critics.

Bell, Goodloe Harper (1832–1899). Pioneer Seventh-day Adventist educator. He started the "Select School" in Battle Creek in 1872 that evolved two years later into *Battle Creek College. Some of his first students included *James Edson White and *W. C. White, the children of James and Ellen G. White, and Dr. *J. H. Kellogg. Despite some behavioral challenges from students, Ellen G. White recognized his fine qualities as a consummate educator and called for church members to support him.

beneficence. The desire to do good to others; related to *benevolence. Ellen G. White describes the "circuit of beneficence" (DA 21).

benevolence. The desire to do good for others; goodwill. Ellen G. White especially liked to use the term **disinterested benevolence* to describe Jesus' unselfish example in coming to this earth (DA 541). In early Adventism, the first method for the support of ministry was called *systematic benevolence* (ca. 1859–1879).

besotted. Intoxicated or drunk. Ellen G. White describes how the "intoxicating cup," referring to alcoholic wine, has a "besotting power." Such inebriation causes the senses to become benumbed (DA 222).

Bible. Ellen G. White believed that the Bible was the very Word of God, the supreme *revelation of His will, and thus the "standard by which all teaching and experience must be tested" (GC vii). "The whole Bible is a manifestation of Christ" (MH 122). As such, the whole world needs to learn about the gospel. "There is a famine for the word of God" (COL 228). The Bible is the "foundation of all true knowledge" (FE 393) and serves as "God's great lesson book" (COL 107). It "is to be our study" and is "an inexhaustible treasure" (COL 109). "This Word, arranged into books, the Old and New Testaments," she explained, "is the guidebook to the inhabitants of a fallen world, bequeathed to them that, by studying and obeying the directions, not one soul would lose its way to heaven" (FLB 10). When approaching the Bible, it is vital not to make it "vindicate your own opinions." It can only be properly understood "by those who are humbly seeking for a knowledge of the truth that they may obey it" (COL 112). "We need the enlightenment of the Holy Spirit in order to discern the truths in God's word" (COL 113). Her view of the Bible is succinctly stated: "The Bible is God's voice speaking to us, just as surely as though we could hear it with our ears. If we realized this, with what awe would we open God's word, and with what earnestness would we search its precepts! The reading and contemplation of the Scriptures would be regarded as an audience with the Infinite One" (6T 393). She also warned that part of Satan's snare at the end of time is to undermine and deny the divine origin of the Bible (GC 557).

Bible Conference, 1919. The first significant dialogue

about the *authority of Ellen G. White's writings after her death in 1915. The *conference was held at Washington Missionary College (now Washington Adventist University) July 1–19, 1919, for the express purpose of bringing doctrinal unity so that Adventists could call greater attention to their beliefs. Although not originally slated, as issues came up, delegates appealed to Ellen G. White's writings to help settle doctrinal differences. During the Bible conference, the topic of Ellen G. White's prophetic ministry came up twice and then was discussed in depth during the postconference meeting with history and Bible teachers. Educators expressed concerns about a rigid and literal view of inspired writings and held that such a view did not accurately reflect her as those present knew her (especially since the concept of *inerrancy clearly did not fit her practice, as she revised her writings repeatedly throughout her lifetime). Unfortunately, such discussions never reached a conclusion nor were any recommendations implemented.

Bible institute. A small convention of ministers, teachers, colporteurs, and their spouses gathered for a period of intense Bible study. They typically lasted anywhere from two to eight weeks, with classes led by prominent church leaders, most notably Uriah Smith and J. N. Loughborough. Bible institutes were frequently referenced during the 1870s through the 1890s.

black Americans, work for. Race relations was the dominant issue in nineteenth-century America as Americans were polarized over the issue of slavery with significant discrimination against blacks in the South that continued through the Reconstruction and Jim Crow era. The issue of slavery was only resolved after a bloody Civil War (1861–1865). Ellen G. White strongly supported abolitionist attempts to free slaves. During the outbreak of hostilities, she had a vision in Parkville, Michigan, on January 12, 1861, in which she was shown that there would be some who would lose sons in the war. At the time, popular sentiment suggested that this would be a short conflict, but it lasted four years. She described the conflict as God's punishment for the evil of slavery. During the Reconstruction period (1865–1877), she advocated for the uplifting of black Americans in the South. As a response, her son *James Edson White did missionary work on the boat *The Morning Star*. These and related efforts culminated in the birth of a school known today as Oakwood University.

Bourdeau, Augustin Cornelius (1834–1916). Early Seventh-day Adventist minister born in Saint Armand, Lower Canada (now Quebec); brother of *D. T. Bourdeau. Originally a Baptist, he converted in 1856 and was ordained to the ministry in 1857. In 1862, he helped to organize the Vermont Conference, and later he served as president of the Quebec Conference. He traveled to Europe in 1884, returned in 1888, and resumed ministry in Canada and New England.

Bourdeau, Daniel T. (1835–1905). Early Seventh-day Adventist minister born in Enosburg Falls, Vermont; brother of *A. C. Bourdeau. In 1868, he went to California with *J. N. Loughborough but returned in 1870 to evangelize French-speaking immigrants in Wisconsin and Illinois. In 1876, he joined *J. N. Andrews in Switzerland for a year. He returned to Europe again in 1883, where he stayed until 1887. While in Europe, he had a falling out with Ellen G. White over missionary methods, but ultimately he heeded her warnings.

braggadocio spirit. Someone who has a tendency to brag (3T 459).

broadside. A large piece of paper printed on one side. Some of Ellen G. White's earliest visions were printed in this format.

brook. To bear, endure, or support. Ellen G. White described some people who received a slight that they could not brook (PP 611). Similarly, she described young men who advised Rehoboam that he should deal sternly with his subjects and that "he would brook no interference with his personal wishes" (PK 89).

Brownsberger, Sidney (1845–1930). Adventist educator. He was active in the development of *Battle Creek College and later *Healdsburg College (now Pacific Union College). Before arriving in Healdsburg, California, he experienced a turbulent divorce.

Butler, George Ide (1834–1918). Adventist minister and administrator originally from Vermont. His parents were active in the *Millerite revival and early Sabbatarian Adventist movement. In 1853, he relocated to Iowa, where he was converted and briefly taught school. In 1865, after the defection of B. F. Snook and W. H. Brinkerhoff, he was elected as president of the Iowa Conference and received a ministerial license two years later. He was a strong supporter of Ellen G. White's prophetic ministry. In 1872, due to *James White's failing health, he was elected General Conference president (until 1874 when James White resumed the post). In 1880, he again became General Conference president. During the *General Conference Session of 1888, he opposed *E. J. Waggoner and *A. T. Jones but later repented for his hardness of heart. Shortly after the session, he had a serious health setback and relocated to a citrus farm in Florida. The next year his wife, Lentha, suffered a debilitating stroke. In

1901, after her death, he was elected president of the Florida Conference and then later as the first president of the Southern Union. In 1907, he married Elizabeth Work Grainger.

Byington, John (1798–1887). Adventist minister, abolitionist, and first president of the General Conference of Seventh-day Adventists. Originally a Deist, he was converted in 1816 at a Methodist camp meeting. Afterward he became a circuit-riding preacher. His convictions against slavery motivated his departure from the Methodist Episcopal Church to help form the Wesleyan Methodist Church. He joined the Liberty Party (the first truly antislavery political organization) and the Free-Soil Party (opposed to the spread of slavery in new territories west of the Mississippi River). He named three of his sons after prominent abolitionists. He converted to Sabbatarian Adventism in 1852 after reading a copy of the **Review and Herald* at his home in Bucks Bridge, New York. He continued to serve as a circuit-riding minister dividing his time between ministering to groups of believers and working on the farm—this enabled him to support himself so that he never drew a salary from the denomination and also allowed him to give generously to support church projects. Five years later, he relocated to Michigan to help combat fanaticism. In October 1862, he was granted ministerial ordination. The next year he was elected as the first (and oldest) president of the General Conference. Although Ellen White did admonish him, he is notable because he is the only church president she did not rebuke for abuse of power. He deeply respected and promoted the prophetic gift within the denomination, including requiring ministerial candidates to affirm the gift of prophecy. During his administration, he organized ministers into districts and encouraged congregations to build meetinghouses. Deeply loved by many church members, he was known as "the praying president" (see Brian E. Strayer, *John Byington: First General Conference President, Circuit-Riding Preacher, and Radical Reformer* [Nampa, ID: Pacific Press®, 2017], 172).

C

caligraph/calligraph. An early version of the typewriter. Ellen White incorrectly spelled it with two *L*'s (Lt. 19c, 1892).

calumny. False or defamatory statements. The **Review and Herald* would sometimes carry warnings against "calumniators," urging people to mind their own business and not condemn anyone unheard (RH Feb. 15, 1870).

Calvin, John (1509–1564). *Protestant Reformer based chiefly in Geneva, Switzerland. Ellen G. White described him as one of the great heroes of the faith in the *great controversy between Christ and Satan. Calvin shaped his theological ideas around what modern interpreters describe as TULIP: total depravity of humanity, unlimited *grace, limited *atonement, irresistible grace, and perseverance of the saints. Some of his later adherents are known as *Puritans; a portion of whom traveled to the United States to seek religious asylum. His name is often associated with Reformed denominations, such as various Dutch and German Reformed churches and the Congregationalist, Baptist, and Presbyterian Churches.

camp meeting. A general gathering, often held on a farm or in a grove of trees, with attendees sleeping in tents. The center of the camp meeting was the speaker's stand with benches. In some places, a large tent was erected to protect from bad weather and the cold. Early camp meetings were primarily evangelistic in nature.

Canright, Dudley Marvin (1840–1919). Adventist minister who joined the denomination in 1859, was ordained in 1865, and traveled widely as a minister. He authored numerous articles and books and was a close friend of James and Ellen G. White. After the death of his first wife, Lucretia Cranson, in 1879, his relationship with the *church grew uncertain. He left the denomination permanently and on March 5, 1887, joined the Otsego, Michigan, Baptist Church, which gave him a license to preach. He later became an outspoken critic of Ellen G. White's prophetic ministry and the Seventh-day Adventist Church.

canvasser. A term used to describe a colporteur or literature evangelist; someone who distributes literature by selling a variety of print materials door to door. "The canvassing work," Ellen G. White wrote, "properly conducted, is missionary work of the highest order" (CEv 5).

carnival. A circus or large festive occasion. Ellen G. White warned against constantly seeking pleasure and making life merely a grand carnival (MH 91).

caste. Social division based on rank, privilege, or race. Ellen White was clearly against any form of this practice and used the term frequently. She was emphatic that "no distinction on account of nationality, race, or caste, is recognized by God" (COL 386). "He who is closely connected with Christ is lifted above the prejudice of color or caste" (9T 209).

cavil. Petty or unnecessary objections. Ellen G. White described those who "cavil at the words of Christ"—especially the Pharisees (DA 241; cf. DA 267, 455).

chaplet. A term used for the wreath placed upon the

Olympic champion during the ancient Olympic Games. Ellen G. White described a "chaplet of fading laurel" (AA 311).

character. The "thoughts and feelings combined," according to Ellen G. White, "make up the moral character" (5T 310). A "properly balanced character" consists of the development of the physical, mental, and spiritual dimensions for each human being (4T 197, 198). "The path of the just is progressive" (3T 542); therefore, character development, or *sanctification, is the *work of a lifetime (4T 367). Ellen G. White noted that "to learn of Christ means to receive His grace, which is His character" (COL 271). True Christian character is a lifelong goal that is to "be reached" (Ed 18). The harvest of life is character, which determines our destiny (Ed 109; MB 90); "it is character that decides destiny" (COL 74). In one of Ellen G. White's often-referenced quotations, she described this concept of character: "The greatest want of the world is the want of men—men who will not be bought or sold, men who in their inmost souls are true and honest, . . . men whose conscience is as true to duty as the needle to the pole, men who will stand for the right though the heavens fall" (Ed 57).

Christian courtesy. A Christian *virtue that, according to Ellen G. White, every Christian should exhibit to show kind respect for others.

Christology. Ellen G. White believed in the eternally divine person and *work of Jesus Christ, especially on Earth. It is therefore Jesus Christ who is the divine hope that spans across all ages. "Christ is the truth," she wrote (COL 110). Jesus Christ is a central theme that spans from the beginning to the end of Ellen G. White's prophetic ministry. While some during her lifetime sought to put Ellen G.

White on a pedestal, she repeatedly and consistently urged people to look to Jesus (2T 118, 119).

church. The church is the body of believers. Thus the corporate experience, what Ellen G. White often referred to as being "in meeting," was what was important, not the actual building (3T 518). Especially up through the 1880s, a church building was frequently referred to as a "meetinghouse." Adventist meetinghouses were to be orderly and well-built (2T 256, 257). Ellen G. White believed that as a corporate body, the Seventh-day Adventist Church is God's remnant church, and despite flaws, will eventually "come to port," to describe a shipping metaphor that it will finally reach the culmination of prophetic significance when Jesus Christ returns. While the church was flawed, she considered it to be a sin to purposefully embarrass the "weakness of Seventh-day Adventists" (2T 106, 109). Each church member should come into proper *church relation. She also admonished that individual church members are not free to advocate whatever views one chooses, irrespective of the judgment of the church (2T 450, 451). Ellen White's most significant statement on the church reads thus: "Enfeebled and defective as it may appear, the church is the one object upon which God bestows in a special sense His supreme regard. It is the theater of His grace, in which He delights to reveal His power to transform hearts" (AA 12). *See also* remnant people.

church discipline. *See* trials; ecclesiology.

church organization. *See* organization, church.

church relationship/relation. Ellen G. White "made plain" the "obligation of church relationship," in which each Christian has a sacred *duty to interact and engage with one another in Christian fellowship (Ed 268). Every committed Christian should be an active member of a local church congregation and thus develop meaningful Christian relationships that will extend from this Earth into heaven. Thus, the work of salvation "is accomplished through the church" (COL 70).

church scavengers. A phrase used by Ellen G. White to describe those who gossip and backbite at church (4T 194). Such persons, unless they repent and are converted, will not see heaven.

churlish. Rude and selfish behavior, depicted in the behavior of the biblical character Nabal in his treatment of David and his men (PP 664). *See also* niggardly.

cider bibber. Apple cider can become fermented, and Ellen G. White described those who were addicted to this low-grade alcohol as a "cider bibbers" (5T 354).

cities. Sweeping social changes characterized the *Victorian era. America rapidly changed from a culture dominated by small towns and the countryside to one shaped by cities and suburbs. Waves of "uprooted" immigrants, together with rapid industrialization, created virtually insurmountable urban problems. Industrialization, with the drive for efficiency, contributed to the lessening of moral restraints and created new ethical, social, labor, and political problems. Ellen G. White warned about cities as places of *vice, often focused on pleasure and amusement, similar to the biblical Sodom and Gomorrah (COL 54). At the same time, Christ died to save all human beings, and this meant that it was essential for *evangelism to be done in the cities in preparation for Christ's soon return (e.g., COL 234).

clarity of Scripture. *See* perspicuity of Scripture.

colaborers. A phrased used by Ellen G. White to describe the process of *sanctification. Throughout the Christian journey, every individual believer must be a "colaborer" with Christ. As a result, the Christian is led to do good and save souls (4T 615).

college home. A school dormitory. In one instance, Ellen G. White recorded having dinner with students at the "college home" in South Lancaster, Massachusetts (Ms 42, 1890).

College of Medical Evangelists. Ellen White was closely involved in the purchase of a property in 1906 that became "not only a sanitarium, but also an educational center" (RH June 21, 1906, in MM 56). Today it is known as Loma Linda University.

common level. A common phrase typically contrasted with the "sacredness of the work" (4T 186). Ellen G. White sometimes used the term in conjunction with either Adventist beliefs or lifestyle practices to contrast the ways of the world with that of the "Bible standard" or "gospel standard." Christians should never lower themselves on a "level with the common" (2SAT 72). Instead, "the Christian standard is high and exalted" (4T 37). "God's standard of man is elevated to the highest meaning of the term" (4T 520). Believers should not compare themselves with other believers because the one and only true Example is Jesus Christ.

concert. Ellen G. White used this *Victorian verb to indicate the contrivance of a plan; for example, "Absalom secretly sent picked men . . . to concert measures for a revolt" (PP 730). It also meant to work together, to cooperate closely.

Confederacy. The league of eleven Southern states that

seceded from the American Union in 1860 and fought against the Northern states during the Civil War to defend their way of life and slavery. Ellen G. White was a staunch Northerner (from the northern part of the United States at that time) who opposed the Confederacy and slavery. (see Jud Lake, *A Nation in God's Hands*). Ellen G. White seems to make subtle allusions to the Confederacy when she describes Satan's agents who "confederated with evil men" (DA 760). Similarly, she describes the "half-and-half service" of Christians "who claim to be soldiers of Christ" but instead are really "with the confederacy of Satan" (MB 94).

conference. A general meeting or session of an organization; also used to describe a grouping of churches.

Conflict of the Ages series. A series of books expounding on the biblical and historical narrative surrounding the *great controversy theme. This series of books initially began in *Spiritual Gifts*, volumes 1–4 (1858–1864), *The Spirit of Prophecy*, volumes 1–4 (1870–1884), and finally, in its most complete form, was published as five books: *Patriarchs and Prophets* (1890), *Prophets and Kings* (1917), *The Desire of Ages* (1898), *The Acts of the Apostles* (1911), and *The Great Controversy* (1888, 1907, 1911).

connection. Usually used to describe an association, such as a "church connection," that indicates church membership. Ellen G. White also used the term in the sense of the literary context of her writings (1SM 44).

conscience. The ability to discern between right and wrong. Those who appease the conscience, or those who give a little to appease the conscience but who do not live a consistent life, are in grave danger (2T 238). While those who ignore the conscience are on one extreme, there are others who have too tender a conscience.

conversion. The experience of faith in Christ and *repentance through which the heart is awakened and the believer responds to Him in *faith. "God's plan," wrote Ellen G. White, "is first to reach the heart" (MH 157). She, from her *Methodist background, emphasized the individual choice of every believer in this process. The ongoing walk of the believer after conversion is described as *sanctification. This continuing process is not the *work of a moment but that of a lifetime.

Cornell, Merritt E. (1827–1893). Adventist minister from Michigan who adopted the *Sabbath in 1852. In 1854, he held the first Sabbatarian Adventist tent meetings with *J. N. Loughborough. In 1855, he joined *Joseph Bates and *J. H. Waggoner as part of a committee of three who prepared an address for the 1855 General Conference Session. This address on spiritual gifts marked a turning point in building confidence in Ellen G. White's prophetic gift. During his lifetime, she sent him a number of important admonitions.

Cottrell, Roswell F. (1814–1892). Adventist minister and administrator who came from a Seventh Day Baptist family. He became a Sabbatarian Adventist in 1851 and later traveled widely and wrote copiously in Adventist publications.

courtship. A term used by Ellen G. White to indicate an exclusive relationship in preparation for *marriage.

covenant theology. Also known as *federal theology*, this is a biblical theology that emphasizes that God relates to His creatures through covenants—binding relationships between God and humanity. Covenant theology was especially prevalent among the *Puritans and was extremely popular in nineteenth-century American religion. Ellen G. White uses language from covenant theology to describe the *law of God. She considered Seventh-day Adventists as *modern Israel, who had much to learn from ancient Israel.

covert. Something that is hidden, covered, or private. Ellen G. White warns not to "for one moment give place to an impure, covert suggestion" (CH 626) from Satan.

covetousness. A common term used to describe selfishness as an unlawful desire to possess some illegitimate thing. One of Ellen G. White's strongest warnings against covetousness can be found in volume 3 of *Testimonies for the Church* (544–551). She equated the sin of covetousness with that of idolatry (PP 439). At one point, she defined the term as the desire to grasp for more and more, which is a characteristic of those who worship "the god of this world," *mammon (PK 63, 64). She furthermore stated that this is the most common sin and is "the most lightly regarded" (PP 496).

craven. Contemptibly lacking in courage; a coward. Used as in a "craven spirit" (DA 218).

credulity. A tendency to readily believe something that is not true (DA 59).

criticism. Ellen G. White warned against a critical spirit. The work of judging and condemning should be left with God (MB 58). *See also* trials.

Crosier, Owen Russell Loomis (1820–1912). Millerite

preacher and editor from Canandaigua, New York. He is best remembered for collaborating with *Hiram Edson to publish their views about the cleansing of the *sanctuary.

cumberer of the ground. A *Victorian expression with roots traceable to Middle English and Celtic; refers to weeds growing in a garden patch. Ellen G. White used the expression in the context of being spiritually weighed down or hampered (5T 139, 185).

C

cupidity. Greed for money or possessions (5T 202). This was Solomon's downfall (PK 72).

cut and slash. The improper use of Ellen G. White's writings by those who in their "zeal for the *Testimonies*" manifest "more self-righteousness than humility" (2T 20). Ellen G. White emphasized instead that individuals should focus on how to apply such *Testimonies* to themselves rather than to point out the faults of others in a critical way.

Czechowski, Michael Belina (1818–1876). Polish Adventist missionary and minister. Originally trained to become a Roman Catholic priest, he became an Adventist in 1857. He subsequently worked among French-speaking Canadians and New Englanders. In 1864, he tried to convince the church leaders to send him as a missionary, but they did not acquiesce due to some concerns. Instead, he convinced the Advent Christian Church to sponsor him, although he continued to teach Seventh-day Adventist *doctrines. Thus, he became the first unofficial missionary to work in Switzerland. Later, some of his converts contacted the church leaders, which led to the sending of *J. N. Andrews as the first official denominational missionary in 1874.

D

daguerreotype. An early photographic process that was popular in the United States during the 1850s and 1860s. The process exposed a picture on a piece of silvered metal, usually copper. Ellen G. White used the term as a metaphor: "The word of God is to us a daguerreotype of the mind of God and of Christ" (3T 538).

Dammon (also Damman, Damon), Israel (1811–1886). A Millerite who was an early supporter of Ellen G. Harmon's ministry in early 1845. He was twice arrested for disturbing the peace on different occasions. The first instance resulted in a trial in 1845. He later claimed to have received a vision and rejected Ellen's ministry. In 1874, *Miles Grant used the Israel Dammon incident to undermine the credibility of Ellen G. White's ministry, but *D. M. Canright dismissed Dammon as a *fanatic whose followers had disrupted his own evangelistic *work in Maine. Even after Canright's later apostasy, with all of his systematic attacks against Ellen G. White's prophetic ministry, he did not believe the incident of Dammon's trial as credible enough to use in his own assaults against Ellen G. White's prophetic ministry.

Daniells, Arthur Grosvenor (1858–1935). Adventist minister and administrator. He worked with *R. M. Kilgore in Texas beginning in 1878. He served briefly as a literary assistant to James and Ellen G. White. He later served as an evangelist in New Zealand in 1886. After moving to Australia, he again worked closely with Ellen G. White. In 1901, he led a bold move to reorganize the General Conference and was afterward elected president of the General Conference, a position he held until 1922. He played a pivotal role—after Ellen G. White's death—in the *1919 Bible Conference. He strongly affirmed

Ellen G. White's prophetic ministry: "It is my deep conviction that Mrs. White's life far transcends the life of anyone I have ever known or with whom I have been associated. . . . I never once heard her boast of the gracious gift God had bestowed upon her, or of the marvelous results of her endeavors. She did rejoice in the fruitage, but gave all the glory to Him who wrought through her" (Arthur G. Daniells, *The Abiding Gift of Prophecy* [Mountain View, CA: Pacific Press®, ca. 1936], 368).

daysman. A mediator. Ellen G. White refers to Jesus as our "Daysman" (DA 25).

death. The cessation of life. Ellen G. White accepted the biblical view that when a person dies, they "sleep," or do not know anything until resurrected by Jesus at the *Second Coming. In this respect, she was sympathetic to the teachings of George Storrs and other Millerites who adopted the nonimmortality of the soul.

declension. A state of deterioration or decline. A term often associated with a spiritual danger. Ellen G. White warned against "spiritual declension," "religious declension," or "moral declension" (GC 253, 260, 279). Ellen G. White sometimes used the term in contrast with the need for spiritual insight (5T 211). Only those who could see things from Heaven's perspective had spiritual insight in contrast to those whose sensibilities were beclouded in "spiritual declension."

Deism. A philosophy that emphasizes that God is not actively involved in the affairs of human beings in this world. Deism became very popular during the time of the American Revolution. *William Miller was a Deist prior to his conversion and subsequent adoption of views about the *Second Coming. Ellen White warned her readers about the "infidel productions" of the deist philosopher Thomas Paine (ST April 21, 1890).

deleterious. Harmful. Workers at the *Battle Creek Sanitarium, for example, were admonished to be aware of their influence and to avoid any "deleterious influence" that might sway them "from the path of right" (4T 562).

dilatory. Slow to act. Ellen G. White warned against those who "delay" or are "even dilatory" before it is too late (4T 343).

disaffection. In the phrase "the poison of disaffection" (4T 195), *disaffection* refers to a rebellious spirit.

discipline. A common term most often referring to *church discipline, or Christian discipline, which was a common way to maintain church order. Another important use of the word related to discipline of children. Such discipline must be redemptive. On the one extreme are parents who neglect discipline, and on the other are parents who are harsh. Neither one, according to Ellen G. White, is condoned by the *Bible. She also spoke about the importance of self-discipline, particularly as related to one's *habits and *character.

discrimination. The act of carefully distinguishing between right and wrong. Ellen White urged believers to have "keen discrimination" (PP 378). Although she never used this term in the sense of racial discrimination, Ellen White spoke often of the concept with the word *caste.

disinterested benevolence. Service to others with no respect to oneself. Jesus is the ultimate model of disinterested benevolence by leaving heaven to come to Earth and die.

dissemblers. People who disguise or conceal themselves

behind false appearances or who disguise their real natures or motives (5T 299). Ellen G. White referred to Achish (1 Sam. 21:11–15; 28:1–2; 29:2–11), who complained as part of those "dissembling" elements (PP 673).

dissipation. Overindulgence in sensual pleasures, or squandering resources, such as money. Ellen G. White compared the time of Noah to the present time in which "the transgressors of God's law are filling the earth with wickedness. Their betting, their horse racing, their gambling, their dissipation, their lustful practices, their untamable passions, are fast filling the world with violence" (DA 633). Similarly, she described how *Martin Luther was horrified at the "dissipation" of the monks and citizens during his visit to Rome (GC 125).

doctrine. The organization of the church's teachings into various theological articles based on the Bible's teaching. Ellen G. White, like most Adventists of her time, cautioned against creeds, yet she was not against the careful articulation of doctrines from Scripture. In contrast with much of the *Protestant world, Ellen G. White rejected tradition and taught that *truth should be adhered to as progressive *light revealed in the *Bible. The earliest statement of Seventh-day Adventist doctrines was articulated by *Uriah Smith in 1872.

domestic wine. A *Victorian term used to describe grape juice that could be slightly fermented. In one instance, Ellen G. White admonished a husband for not giving his pregnant wife enough nutritious food. She said that some "domestic wine" would have helped this woman to get the nutrition that she needed (2T 383).

dress reform. Ellen G. White urged that Seventh-day Adventists "dress plainly"; the garments should be both healthful and devoid of worldly fashions (3T 366, 367). "Fashion is a mistress that rules with an iron hand," she warned (Ed 246). Garments should be free from jewelry and ornaments so as to not attract unnecessary attention. A dress reformer lives by principle rather than by passing fads. At the same time, dress reformers "should seek not to disgust unbelievers by carelessness and slackness in our apparel" (2T 66). Ultimately, *dress reform* is a form of *self-denial that brings glory to God. Extravagance in clothing prevents money from going to those who need help. Christian principles of dress should include being neat, healthful, appropriate, and becoming (Ed 248). Discussing the fashions of her time, Ellen G. White cautioned that women should avoid skirts that sweep the ground or place unnecessary weight on the hips or the chest and thus restrict the internal organs so that there is no room for the lungs to expand (MH 291, 292). Dress reformers should not be controlled by fashion, but instead should "have the courage to dress healthfully and simply" (MH 294).

drudgery. Anything that is burdensome, especially used in conjunction with household *duties. "Nothing is drudgery to the one who submits to the will of God" (9T 150).

drug(s). A broad term in the nineteenth century for any kind of medication. Ellen G. White noted that the majority of drugs available during her lifetime, especially at the time of her *health reform vision in 1863, were poisonous substances prescribed by medical doctors (2SM 276–303). These drugs included alcohol, opium, and cocaine. She commended "simpler remedies" (2SM 279); but as medical science increased, she did not oppose all medications, dietary supplements, or inoculations.

duty/duties. Frequently used in the phrase "sense of duty," this was a well-known term from Ellen G. White's time to indicate responsibility. "Obedience to God is the first duty of the Christian" (4T 610). She felt that it was her duty to share with others what God had revealed to her. At other times, it was out of a sense of duty that she traveled, or even refrained from travel, to certain places. She shared *testimonies, both oral and written, out of a sense of duty, even though it was painful when people spurned the admonition she transmitted. Ellen G. White also described the importance of being faithful in the little duties of life, such as household chores, before a person should be entrusted with larger responsibilities. She also writes that doctrinal *truth, as revealed and once people understand it, becomes "present duty" (2T 429). The term *duty* had moral implications for the Christian believer in the nineteenth century that can be difficult to overestimate. The "law of duty is supreme" for every Christian and must be taken seriously (4T 163). "Spiritual disease" results from the neglect of duty (4T 235, 236). People have no difficulty in understanding duty, Ellen G. White admonished, when it is in harmony with their personal inclinations. Duty becomes plain in the *Bible or as indicated "by circumstances and reason." When seeing a duty, one should not pray to be excused but to humbly submit (PP 440).

dyspeptic/dyspepsia. A term used to describe a person afflicted with indigestion, general stomach discomfort, or an irritable mental state. Ellen G. White noted how *exercise can especially help those with dyspeptic digestive organs (MH 240). She also used the term in a spiritual sense when she describes some people who become "spiritual dyspeptics" (4T 235; cf. 5T 117).

E

early rain. Ellen G. White noted that "in the East the former rain falls at the sowing time" so that the seed may germinate. She compares this to the work of the *Holy Spirit (TM 506), especially at Pentecost (cf. AA 38). *See also* latter rain; revival.

economy. The management, regulation, and government of a family and concerns of the household. It could aslo express the importance of saving money, time, or some other resource. Christians are stewards of these resources, so they should exercise great care in how they invest these resources. Such economy includes the value that parents should place on teaching children "the right use of money." Children should be supplied with money, either by their parents or through their own earnings, so that they learn how to purchase their own necessities and to keep an account of their expenses. In this way, they can learn "true economy" and avoid niggardliness (Ed 239). *See also* niggardly.

Edson, Hiram (1806–1882). Adventist minister who is best remembered for his studies with *O. R. L. Crosier and others about the *sanctuary *doctrine. In 1852, with the proceeds from the sale of his farm, he helped *James White to purchase the Adventists' first printing press in Rochester, New York. He also trained the first Sabbatarian Adventist preachers.

education. Ellen G. White defined true education as "the harmonious development of the physical, the mental, and the spiritual powers" that "prepares the student for the joy of service in this world and for the higher joy of wider service in the world to come" (Ed 13). "Ignorance will not increase the humility or spirituality of any professed follower of Christ," she wrote in 1872, which was the same year that *Goodloe Harper Bell started his first school in Battle Creek, Michigan. "The truths of the divine word can be best appreciated by an intellectual Christian. Christ can be best glorified by those who serve Him intelligently. The great object of education is to enable us to use the powers that God has given us in such a manner as will best represent the religion of the Bible and promote the glory of God" (3T 160; cf. MH 150). The Whites availed themselves of educational opportunities for their children, sponsored other children to obtain such educations, and invested a significant amount of their energy into helping start Adventist schools. Ellen G. White's magnum opus on the philosophy of Adventist education is found in her 1903 work *Education*. "True education," she writes, "is not the forcing of instruction." Instead, "the mental powers must be awakened, the interest aroused" (Ed 41).

effeminate. In the modern sense, *effeminate* is a reference to having feminine characteristics; in the nineteenth century, the term tended to be used in its secondary sense of excessive softness and indulgence. Ellen G. White used it to describe King Solomon's *character, which after his fall, became "enervated and effeminate" (PK 58).

efficacy. The ability to produce a desired or intended result. Ellen G. White stated that we are "cleansed by His efficacy," when describing the saving work of Jesus Christ (DA 646).

electricity. Ellen G. White made a number of references to the practical applications of electricity, which came about during her lifetime. In spiritual terms, she mentions Jesus' humanity being "charged with a heavenly current" (DA 363) or discovering the "current of spiritual strength" (DA 676).

electric physician. A term used to describe a healer who used *mesmerism and hypnosis (5T 198). *See also* animal magnetism.

Ellen G. White Estate Inc. The Ellen G. *White Estate Inc. was set up at the request of the General Conference of Seventh-day Adventists to honor Ellen G. White's wishes for the creation of an organization to preserve and promulgate her writings after her death. It is led by a board of five trustees.

Elmshaven. Ellen G. White's home in California for the last fifteen years of her life (1900–1915). It is located in the Napa Valley, about sixty miles (ninety-seven kilometers) north of San Francisco. The property contained thirty-five acres (fourteen hectares) with various fruit orchards, a barn, and an adjacent office building.

Emancipation Proclamation/papers. The executive order issued by President Abraham Lincoln that freed all slaves on January 1, 1863. Ellen G. White referenced this historical event in connection with the *atonement of Jesus Christ who thereby "signed the emancipation papers of the [human] race" (MH 90).

enervate. A person who is deprived of force or strength; to weaken. "Intemperance of any kind," wrote Ellen White, "will enervate a character originally firm, noble, and independent" (ST Aug, 1, 1878).

erelong. Before a long time had elapsed (PP 647).

erysipelas. A painful bacterial infection caused by streptococcal bacteria entering the skin through cuts or sores. James and Ellen G. White's infant son *John Herbert White tragically died from this disease in 1860.

eschatology. From the Greek word for "last things" (*eschata*); the *doctrine of eschatology deals with final matters, such as the *second coming of Christ and the restoration of the *kingdom of God. Ellen G. White learned about the second coming of Christ when she heard *William Miller preach his revivalist message regarding the soon return of Jesus "about the year 1843" (4SP 206). Although disappointed on October 22, 1844, after her first vision, she believed she had a role to encourage God's people to continue studying the *Bible to learn the source of their disappointment and to renew their hope in the soon return of Jesus Christ. Ellen G. White interpreted events during her lifetime, such as natural disasters, as having eschatological significance as confirmatory signs of the end of time. She furthermore specified eschatological events, such as Sunday laws, that will become flash points that will separate God's people from the world just before the *second advent of Christ.

E

ethics. The moral principles based on the law of God that govern a Christian's behavior. "The ethics inculcated by the gospel," Ellen G. White wrote, "acknowledge no standard but the perfection of God's mind, God's will" (7T 276). She wrote extensively about human *character and behavior and viewed *good works and *sanctification as Spirit-enabled responses through *justification by faith that led to *holiness as revealed through Scripture. She upheld a high view of the *law of God that led to ethical imperatives from Scripture. A high regard for the Ten Commandments also meant a high regard for natural law, including *health reform. *See also* moral philosophy.

evangelicalism. Derived from the Greek word *euangélion*, meaning "good news," the term *evangelical* became associated with the *Protestant Reformation to recover the gospel of Jesus Christ through *faith alone. As a specific movement within Protestantism, evangelicalism arose within the context of eighteenth-century revivalism in Britain and the American colonies. It had deep roots in Pietism and *Puritanism and was influenced heavily by *John Wesley, George Whitefield, and Jonathan Edwards.

evangelism. Ellen G. White believed that sharing one's faith with others was a natural part of the Christian experience. "Real godliness is diffusive and communicative" (3T 543). Christians have a responsibility, not to wait for souls to come to them, but to "seek them out where they are" (COL 229). A variety of approaches is necessary: "Not all can be reached in the same way," she noted (COL 387). She personally felt, in her own experience, that it was her *duty to share her faith, both privately and publicly. She urged Christians to "taste the joy of winning souls" (COL 58). "The success of the gospel message does not depend upon learned speeches, eloquent testimonials, or deep arguments. It depends upon the simplicity of the message and its adaptation to the souls that are hungering for the bread of life" (COL 231). Thus, "studied" words "have but little influence." The most effective way to reach hearts, she urged, is the "true, honest expression . . . spoken in natural simplicity" (COL 232).

execration. The act or object of cursing or exposing something that is to be detested. Ellen G. White describes the apostle Paul, after he was accused of "instigating" the fire that burned much of Rome, as the "object of universal execration" (AA 490).

exercise. A term used to refer to either health or religious exercises (such as reading the *Bible or *prayer). As a major component of *health reform, Ellen G. White tirelessly advocated for the benefits of exercise. "Action is a law of our being," she wrote (MH 237). Inactivity causes disease, whereas exercise increases the circulation of the blood and contributes to health. Such exercise is especially important for "brain workers," and in many instances, exercise is "better for the health than medicine" (MH 238, 240).

experimental religion/knowledge. The practical application of truth. The terms were used by Ellen G. White to describe individuals who have a theoretical knowledge of the *truth but who also need to also apply it to their lives (3T 535; 5T 221). Individuals who do not allow the truth to become an "experimental" part of their everyday lives will not see heaven. Ellen G. White also used the term to describe the role of ministers who must first apply their Bible studies to their own lives before they can hope for their *preaching to be effective and they must relate intellectual truths in a practical way before they can hope to influence their audience.

extremist. *See* fanatic.

eye single to the glory of God. A phrase used by Ellen G. White to emphasize that the sole purpose of the Christian's life is to bring glory to God. She used this phrase hundreds of times in her published writings as well as her *testimonies to remind people to keep a broader perspective about the ultimate purpose of the Christian life. One brief example is when she encouraged people to be thrifty in their use of time and money so that they can have "an eye single to the glory of God" (CS 292).

F

faith. The response of the believer to trust God; it comes about through *conversion. Faith is not based upon any merit but is completely a heart response that leads to an entirely new way of life. "Saving faith is a transaction by which those who receive Christ join themselves in covenant relation with God. Genuine faith is life. A living faith means an increase of vigor, a confiding trust, by which the soul becomes a conquering power" (DA 347).

family. Ellen G. White recognized the importance of family, although in her specific situation sometimes that meant she had to leave her children with others. She stated that this was the "greatest sacrifice" of her life (1T 101). She and *James White tried to make their trips as brief as possible, and as their children grew older, they traveled with their sons. Ellen G. White admonished others who neglected their families. "Your first and most sacred duty is to your family," she wrote (2T 85). Furthermore, parents are to "encourage love in the hearts" of their children (2T 260).

fanatic. A person who exhibits a strong spirit or radical ideas that often lead to wild and extravagant emotion or behavior. Such "one-idea men can see nothing except to press the one thing that presents itself to their minds. . . . There is a conscientiousness that will carry everything to extremes, and make Christian duties as burdensome as the Jews made the observance of the Sabbath. . . . One fanatic, with his strong spirit and radical ideas, who will oppress the conscience of those who want to be right, will do great harm" (HS 212).

fanaticism. Extreme devotion and zeal to a cause that leads to wild and extravagant emotion and behavior. Ellen White spoke of "the desolating effects of fanaticism in Maine" shortly after the *Great Disappointment. The fanatical ones, she wrote, "seemed to think that religion consisted in great excitement and noise" (LS 85). Fanaticism was a phenomenon she frequently encountered throughout her seventy-year prophetic ministry.

fastidious. Very attentive to and concerned about accuracy and detail. Ellen G. White noted that when trying to reach the rich classes that it is not necessary to adopt all of their manners and methods or "fastidious tastes" (MH 213).

faultfinding. A common problem and one of the most prevalent themes in the volumes of *Testimonies for the Church* has to do with individuals who find fault with one another. No Christian should ever be the *conscience for someone else. Ellen G. White noted that some personalities are more prone to a spirit of faultfinding and that such persons should not be permitted to associate with Adventist young people or be allowed to be in church leadership. Ellen G. White was unequivocal: "Constant faultfinding is wrong" (3T 531). *See also* criticism.

fervor. Intense and passionate feeling. Ellen G. White described how David with "wonted [lacked] fervor . . . was able, for the last time, to address his people" (PP 750).

F

fete. A public celebration. Ellen G. White described how early Christians were "often made the chief entertainment at public fetes" (GC 40).

fiction. Ellen G. White warned against fiction, especially sensational novels (MH 445, 446). She warned against any books that distract from God's Word (COL 107). A superficial reading of her statements might lead one to initially conclude that she was against anything that is not factual. Ellen G. White did, however, distinguish between great works of literature—such as John Bunyan's *Pilgrim's Progress*, which she recommended (GC 252)—and cheap, trashy dime novels that were sensational in nature. Such mindless literature does not contribute to Christian *character. She did collect stories, some of them nonfactual that had a moral and uplifting purpose, for the four-volume compilation *Sabbath Readings for the Home Circle*. It is therefore quite clear that Ellen G. White did not use the word *fiction* in the same way that many people do today by meaning something nonfactual. In a 1962 meeting hosted by the General Conference of Seventh-day Adventists Department of Education, a group of thought leaders concluded that when Ellen G. White used the term *fiction* she was speaking in qualitative terms rather than regarding whether or not something happened in space-time history. Her concerns about the nature of such "fiction" included whether it was (1) addictive; (2) sentimental, sensational, erotic, profane, or trashy; (3) escapist, causing readers to revert to a dream world; (4) whether it unfits the mind for serious study; and (5) whether it is time consuming and valueless (Paul T. Gibbs, "Literature in Adventist Schools" [paper presented to an English Teachers' Conference, Southern Missionary College, Collegedale, TN, 1962]).

Fitch, Charles (1805–1844). Millerite minister prominent in western New York and Ohio. He tragically died from pneumonia after becoming chilled following an outdoor baptismal service. His most famous sermon, "Come Out of Her, My People," denounced other churches that ostracized Millerites. This was characteristic, he believed, of the fall of Babylon in Revelation 18:2. Later, after his death, Ellen G. White described seeing him in the earth made new in her first vision.

folk. A nineteenth-century way to refer in a generic sense to relatives or to a community of people.

foolscap. A roughly legal-size piece of paper, typically with a watermark (3BIO 102). This stationery was common in the nineteenth century.

fop/foppish. A term to describe a foolish person who is overly concerned about his or her clothes or appearance (MC 56; 4T 391).

forgive/forgiveness. The act or process of forgiving or being forgiven. Ellen G. White counseled that forgiveness is a vital part of the Christian experience. Each individual must experience Christ's personal forgiveness and extend that spirit of forgiveness to others. "He who refuses to forgive is thereby casting away his own hope of pardon" (COL 247). Those whose "hearts are not broken and humbled on account of sin" become "exacting and unforgiving toward others" (COL 246).

formal religion. The mere outward observance of beliefs, including Sabbath keeping, that lacks an inward *conversion and therefore lacks the proper motivation. All "formal religion is to be dreaded" and avoided at all costs (4T 396).

Foss, Hazen Little (1819–1893). A Millerite who claimed to receive several visions but refused to share them. According to Ellen G. White, Foss believed that these visions had been taken from him and given to her instead. Though possibly true, White never endorsed Foss's claim. Foss was a brother-in-law to Ellen G. White by marrying her older sister, Mary (1821–1912).

Foy, William Ellis (1818–1893). A black Millerite minister who claimed to receive four visions from 1842 to 1844 and who suffered under racial *prejudice. His visions are similar to some of Ellen G. White's earliest visions, and the first two are published in his tract *The Christian Experience of William E. Foy* (1845).

fractious. Divisive. Being "fractious in spirit," including "dwelling upon the dark side, will make you weak and spiritless" (4T 349).

French modistes. A term for dressmakers who made and

sold fashionable French style dresses and hats. Ellen G. White contrasted *dress reform with their fashions (MH 292).

frivolity. A term used by Ellen G. White, often in conjunction with worldliness, to describe aimless pleasure seeking. She decried the "frivolity of young men and young women" whose "minds are filled with nonsense. Their conversation is only empty, vain talk" (AH 407).

froward generation. A reference to the King James Version's prose for Deuteronomy 32:20. *Froward* means someone or something that is difficult; but in this case, meaning a perverse or disobedient group of people. Ellen G. White alluded to this biblical passage when referring to the condition of the world before Christ's soon return, including the change of the Sabbath (PK 185, 186).

Fuller, Nathan (1825–1895). Adventist minister and conference president in New York and Pennsylvania who in 1869 apostatized after several clandestine affairs became known. Ellen G. White's knowledge of Fuller's experience resulted in the publication of her longest extant *testimony in which she stated that her confidence in humanity had been terribly shaken (2T 439–489). He later joined the *Marion Party, an early dissident movement in Iowa.

Fundamentalism. A theologically conservative movement in that emphasizes a literalistic reading of the Scripture. The term *Fundamentalism* refers to a specific American movement that began in the early twentieth century. In 1922, the Baptist pastor Curtis Lee Laws used the term to refer to the historical Fundamentalist controversy that split many Protestant denominations in North America during the 1920s. While there were many points of agreement between Adventism and

Fundamentalism (especially toward the end of Ellen G. White's lifetime), the Protestant Fundamentalist movement coalesced around a series of twelve volumes titled *The Fundamentals: A Testimony to the Truth* (1910–1915). Some Adventist pioneers such as *S. N. Haskell began to assert the *authority of Ellen G. White's writings as a way to interpret the *Bible and promulgated a much more rigid view of *inspiration. Later, participants in the *1919 Bible Conference recognized that the idea of *inerrancy, or that the Bible and Ellen G. White's writings are incapable of any errors, was especially problematic.

G

Gage, William Claggett (1842–1907). Adventist minister, printer, and civic leader. Converted in 1864 through meetings held by *M. E. Cornell, he left his print shop to become Cornell's tent master and song leader. His family relocated to Battle Creek, Michigan, in 1867, and he worked as a foreman at the Review and Herald Publishing Association. Ellen G. White sent him numerous warnings that led to his drifting away from the *church. In 1878, he returned to denominational employment, was ordained in 1881, and the next year (1882) was elected mayor of Battle Creek.

garret. A small, habitable attic or a small and often dismal, or cramped, living space. Ellen G. White described how at the end of time God's people will "come from garrets, from hovels, from dungeons" (GC 650; cf. GC 252).

gat. In the King James Version, the past tense of *get* is "gat." Ellen G. White noted how some people "gat them away" or "gat them" (PP 671, 745).

gay. Nineteenth-century term for happiness and joy (cf.

PP 158, 162). Ellen G. White spoke of the "gaieties of the hour," speaking of immediate happiness (AA 244). She repeatedly noted that Christians should be happy: "There is nothing gloomy in the religion of Jesus" (MB 88).

General Conference Session of 1888. Ellen G. White saw the need for a more Christ-centered focus within Adventism. At that time, she recognized that the *church required a spiritual *revival. She mediated a conflict between two young ministers, *A. T. Jones and *E. J. Waggoner, and *G. I. Butler and *Uriah Smith. Jones and Waggoner challenged what were perceived as established positions about the law in Galatians and the identity of one of the ten kingdoms in Daniel 7. At the actual General Conference session, held in Minneapolis, Minnesota, which began with a series of ministerial meetings, there was a much more Christ-centered message that she felt the denomination needed. Despite initial opposition, Ellen G. White traveled with Jones and Waggoner, who became the most visible preachers in the denomination during the 1890s. Tragically, Jones and Waggoner later left the denomination; but she noted prior to this that should this happen, it would not diminish the importance of their message for the denomination. *See also* righteousness by faith.

general revelation. A theological term used to describe how God relates to humans through creation. While Ellen G. White didn't use this technical term, she did write extensively about God speaking through *nature. Thus, in a broad sense, this *revelation, though marred by sin, is available to everyone and reveals the power of God. General revelation is different from God's *special revelation as revealed through the *Bible. General revelation is not sufficient to obtain a saving knowledge of the plan of redemption. The full self-disclosure of God is found in Scripture and culminates in the person and *work of Jesus Christ.

genial climate. A pleasant climate (DA 252).

gift of prophecy. *See* prophecy, gift of.

glorification. A theological term that describes the moment when, at the *Second Advent, human beings put aside their mortal bodies and through glorification are transformed into their perfect forms; also to represent something as worthy of praise. Ellen G. White generally used the word *glorification* in conjunction with an admonition not to live for "glorification of self" (Ms 82, 1903).

glory, glory, glory. A common phrase from the Second Great Awakening that was used during *revival meetings. Ellen G. White was known to use this phrase on a number of occasions when she received a vision (1BIO 275).

G

Godhead. A term derived from Colossians 2:9 to describe the essence of the Deity; commonly used as a collective expression for the Father, the Son, and the *Holy Spirit. Many early Sabbatarian Adventists held Arian or semi-Arian views of the Godhead. Such anti-Trinitarian views were particularly common within the Christian Connection and similar restorationist groups. Many of these groups rejected the full Trinity of the Godhead because it was simply equated with Roman Catholic teaching and therefore tantamount to heresy. Early Seventh-day Adventists, most notably H. Camden Lacey (1871–1950), brought awareness of this topic and contributed to a new appreciation for the role of the Holy Spirit and the full divinity of Jesus Christ. Ellen G. White strongly affirmed the eternal preexistence of Jesus Christ and the full personhood of the Holy Spirit. In and after 1897, she made some of her clearest statements about Christ's divinity—"in Christ is life, original, unborrowed, underived"—and in 1896, she also identified the Holy Spirit as "the Third Person of the Godhead" (DA 530, 671). As Seventh-day Adventists saw a strong biblical basis for the three full members of the Godhead, the denomination moved to a strongly Trinitarian position as evidenced by the statements of Fundamental Beliefs (1931, 1980).

God is love. Based on 1 John 4:8, God's *love, or the phrase "God is love," is one of the most prevalent phrases and theological themes of Ellen G. White's writings. This phrase is the opening line of *Patriarchs and Prophets* (the first book in the *Conflict of the Ages series) as well as the last line of *The Great Controversy* (the final book in the same series).

go forward. This phrase was the watchword of the United States in the nineteenth century as Americans migrated westward. Ellen G. White used and adapted this popular phrase in connection with the children of Israel when describing the need of Adventists to recognize that they were on a similar journey, except they were headed to the heavenly Canaan land (4T 26).

good works. *See* works, human.

gospel whip. When biblical teaching is used in a negative way to whip someone into shape. Ellen White applied this term to those who exhibit a *faultfinding spirit toward others (3T 108).

grace. The free, unmerited favor of God. Ellen G. White insisted that grace was through *faith alone (*sola gratia*) and that salvation could not be obtained on the basis of *human works or merit. "We ourselves owe everything to God's free grace," she stated. "Grace in the covenant ordained our adoption. Grace in the Saviour effected our redemption, our regeneration, and our exaltation to heirship with Christ. Let this grace be revealed to others" (COL 250).

Grace is necessary throughout the Christian experience, beginning with *conversion and continuing on in the life through *sanctification.

Grant, Miles (1819–1911). Advent Christian leader and editor of the *World's Crisis*. In 1868, he first met James and Ellen G. White on a train ride. Their initial encounter led to optimistic hope on the part of *James White of a friendship, but their attendance at an Advent Christian *camp meeting the next summer disavowed them of such hopes. Grant later became a fierce critic of Seventh-day Adventists and especially of Ellen G. White's prophetic ministry.

grease. The fat drippings from meat. It should not be confused with vegetable oil. "A plain diet, free from spices and flesh meats and grease of all kinds, would prove a blessing" (2T 45).

great controversy. The spiritual conflict between Christ and Satan over the character of God. It is the dominant motif of Ellen G. White's writings that advances the idea that throughout history the world has been the field on which the great battle between Christ and His *angels and Satan and his angels have fought. While this battle has cosmic implications, it also affects every human being who ever lived on planet Earth. In March 1858, Ellen G. White received a far-reaching vision that unmasked the schemes of Satan and that emphasized the plan of salvation to restore fallen humanity. A key aspect of this great controversy narrative is the perspective of God in terms of the *moral government of God. The death of Jesus Christ exposed to the universe the terrible results of sin. "The cross is a revelation to our dull senses of the pain that, from its very inception, sin has brought to the heart of God" (Ed 263). As part of God's plan of government, He does not use force (COL 77). Instead, Satan is the deceiver.

> When he sinned in heaven, even the loyal angels did not fully discern his [Satan's] character. This was why God did not at once destroy Satan. Had He done so, the holy angels would not have perceived the justice and love of God. A doubt of God's goodness would have been as evil seed that would yield the bitter fruit of sin and woe. Therefore the author of evil was spared, fully to develop his character. Through long ages God has borne the anguish of beholding the work of evil, He has given the infinite Gift of Calvary, rather than leave any to be deceived (COL 72).

What ultimately matters is that God's people demonstrate "loyalty to our Redeemer" (COL 97). In the end, Christ will triumph over evil, and all the inhabitants of the universe will enjoy peace and tranquility throughout the ceaseless ages of eternity.

Great Disappointment. A term used to describe the aftermath when Jesus Christ did not return as anticipated on October 22, 1844. It is sometimes described as the "bitter disappointment" (GC 374). Ellen G. White often referred to this experience as the *"passing of the time" (LS 64).

Griggs, Frederick (1867–1952). Adventist educator who served as the principal of the preparatory school of *Battle Creek College from 1890 to 1899. From 1899 to 1907, he was the principal of the South Lancaster Academy and from 1910 to 1914, he was the president of Union College. He later resumed his educational leadership as the president of Emmanuel Missionary College (1918–1925) and served in a variety of other administrative posts.

groggery. A slightly disreputable establishment for the serving of alcohol (Ed 218).

groove. A term used by Ellen G. White to describe how people who are narrow-minded have such tunnel vision that they can only see things their way, or in a certain groove (4T 129).

gruel. A light food made by boiling flour, oatmeal, and/or other grains together in water or milk to create a thin *porridge. This was a common staple in the White household throughout her lifetime (4T 299). In nineteenth-century British work houses, an onion was also added to the gruel to give vitamins.

H

habit(s). Repeated action that results in a disposition. Ellen G. White cautioned against resisting the *Holy Sprit when God convicts the heart. Gradually, through repeated resistance, "the conviction of duty wears away, and known transgression of God's commandments becomes habit. . . . The heart is hardened, the conscience seared" (COL 279). *See also* Character.

hardihood. Boldness and daring. Ellen G. White described the people at the end of time who oppose God's followers immediately before the *Second Advent, as those who are absorbed in "infidel hardihood" (GC 603).

Haskell, Stephen Nelson (1833–1922). Adventist minister who was an Adventist Christian until he accepted the seventh-day *Sabbath in 1853. Ordained in 1870, he served in a variety of administrative and missionary posts. He was a close friend and confidant of Ellen G. White. In his later life, he proposed *marriage to her, but she politely declined and introduced him to Hetty Hurd, who becamse his second wife.

Healdsburg College. A coeducational boarding school operated in Healdsburg, California, from 1882 to 1908. Ellen White was actively involved in the founding of the college, which eventually moved to a rural location and was renamed Pacific Union College.

health reform. Adherence to a healthy lifestyle that leads to the restoration of the whole person and forms a branch "of the great work which is to fit a people for the coming of the Lord" (CT 9). Ellen G. White believed that natural law was just as important as God's law, particularly the Ten Commandments. "Health is a great treasure" (3T 150). Christians who "violate the laws of their being . . . must pay the penalty by suffering disease" (2T 536). Health "is the reward of obedience to the laws of God" (DA 824). Conversely, "disease is an effort of nature to free the system from conditions that result from a violation of the laws of health" (MH 127). "Pure air, sunlight, abstemiousness, rest, exercise, proper diet, the use of water, trust in divine power—these are the true remedies" (MH 127). Christians therefore have a sacred responsibility to follow health reform because "heaven is all health" (3T 172).

Health Reform Institute. An Adventist medical institution founded in Battle Creek, Michigan, in 1866 as the Western Health Reform Institute. The word *Western* was quickly dropped after its opening as the western frontier in the United States continued to expand. The Health Reform Institute was the forerunner of the *Battle Creek Sanitarium.

Henry, Sarepta Myrenda (Irish) (1839–1900). A leader in the Woman's Christian Temperance Union, she converted to the Seventh-day Adventist Church while she was a patient at the *Battle Creek Sanitarium. She developed a women's and family ministry in the Seventh-day Adventist Church.

Hewitt, David (1805–1878). A tinsmith and peddler from Battle Creek, Michigan, who accepted the seventh-day *Sabbath as presented by *Joseph Bates in 1852 after Bates inquired about who was the "most honest man in town" (6BIO 438). During a meeting held on October 1, 1860, Hewitt moved that the *church's name should be *Seventh-day Adventist.*

Himes, Joshua Vaughan (1805–1895). Millerite minister and publisher. At the age of eighteen, he joined the Christian Connexion church in New Bedford, Massachusetts, and was licensed as an exhorter. In 1825, he was ordained to the ministry. He served in a variety of districts until he met *William Miller and asked him to preach at the Chardon Street Chapel in Boston. Convinced of the *Second Advent, Himes devoted his energies to sharing the message. He published and edited the first Millerite serial publication—the *Signs of the Times*—organized *camp meetings, published thousands of copies of books and pamphlets, and was a close friend and confidant of Miller. After the *Great Disappointment, he led out in the pivotal Albany Conference that rejected the seventh-day *Sabbath and the manifestation of the *gift of prophecy. In 1863, he accepted conditional immortality and joined the Advent Christian Church but later left the movement after a power struggle with *Miles Grant. In his later years, he served as an itinerant priest for the Episcopal denomination in the Dakota Territory.

holy/holiness. A divine attribute that signifies the purity and majesty of God, both in His triune essence and in His actions toward creation. The holiness of any part of creation is dependent upon its unique relation to the Holy God. By *grace and through *faith, the *church, as well as the individual believer, is declared holy. The Christian process of growth in grace (*sanctification) is the daily outworking of the *Holy Spirit in which people are set apart from the world.

holy flesh movement. Term used to describe a holiness *revival centered in Indiana from 1899 to 1900 that contained charismatic experiences. Local leaders expounded on the theological ideas of *A. F. Ballenger that emphasized sinless perfection. Ellen G. White warned against such *fanaticism.

Holy Spirit. A divine Member of the *Godhead, which also includes God the Father and the Son, Jesus Christ. The work of the Holy Spirit is to convict people of sin (MB 7). Ellen G. White also described the gift of the Holy Spirit as "the greatest of all gifts" (MB 132). *See also* Godhead.

home circle/influence. Ellen G. White described the *home circle* or *home influence* as the sacred environs of the *family. The parents are spiritual leaders who should ensure that family worship occurs every morning and evening. Everyone in the family has a *duty to assist with chores, and in particular, husbands should do whatever they can to help lighten the cares of the wife or mother. These home duties "lie at the very foundation of society" (4T 522).

hothouse. During the nineteenth century, *hothouses*, or greenhouses, began to become more common in the United States. Ellen G. White compared Christians who do not exercise their *faith to spindly plants in a hothouse (5T 183).

Hull, Moses (1836–1907). Adventist minister who joined the fledgling Sabbatarian Adventist movement in 1857 but defected to *spiritualism in 1863.

human sympathy. The ability of people to show that they care for someone else. "When human sympathy is blended with love and benevolence, and sanctified by the Spirit of Jesus, it is an element which can be productive of great good" (4T 56).

human will. Ellen White believed like *John Wesley that after man's fall into sin the human will was, by the prevenient grace of God, capable of responding to God. Prevenient grace is God's universal work of grace extended to all humanity to draw them to Him. This universal work of the Holy Spirit prepares the hearts of men and women to accept God's offer of salvation while at the same time never forcing them. They are free to reject the offer of salvation. "What you need to understand" she wrote, "is the true force of the will. This is the governing power in the nature of man, the power of decision, or of choice. Everything depends on the right action of the will. The power of choice God has given to men; it is theirs to exercise" (SC 48). In teaching this, Ellen White departed from *John Calvin's understanding of irresistible grace (DA 466).

human works. *See* works, human.

I

humors. Most often used in reference to moisture or bodily fluids; or a skin disease or cutaneous eruption, or to a disposition, turn of mind, or *temper, since in antebellum America people viewed the mind as dependent upon bodily fluids. Ellen G. White, for example, connected the consumption of "flesh-meats" as bringing about through the blood "cancerous and scrofulous humors" (CE 176).

I

idlers. Those who are lazy and who accomplish little or nothing. "Bible religion never makes men idlers" (MH 195).

illimitable. Without limits or an end. Ellen G. White described how at the close of the *great controversy sin will be no more and that "from Him who created all, flow life and light and gladness, throughout the realms of illimitable space" (GC 678).

illy. A term Ellen G. White used nineteen times in her published writings and consistently used it as an adverb to indicate scarcely or poorly. Examples include "illy prepared" or "illy harmonizes" (3SG 19; 4T 250).

importunate. An adjective meaning persistent to the point of annoyance or intrusion. Ellen G. White describes Jacob's trial as a model for God's people at the end of time as they will need to partake of "importunate prayer" (GC 621).

improvident. Lacking foresight or thoughtless (DA 560).

inculcate. To impress upon by frequent admonitions or to urge upon the mind (PP 717).

indolence. Avoiding activity or exertion, laziness. Ellen G. White stated, "We can never be saved in indolence and inactivity" (COL 280).

inerrancy. The idea that the *Bible and Ellen G. White's writings are free of any error(s). Ellen G. White made it clear that both the Bible and her writings have minor discrepancies in details that do not pertain to the focal message of *revelation that was transmitted by the human messenger (see 1SM 38, 39). *See* revelation and inspiration.

Ings, William (1835–1897) and **Jeannis "Jenny" "Jennie" L.** (1841–1921). Early church workers; Jenny served as a literary assistant to Ellen G. White. In 1876, William was sent to Switzerland to assist *J. N. Andrews, and later they served in England as missionaries with *J. N. Loughborough. In 1882, Ellen G. White urged their return to America where he could assist her with her publications and Jenny could be her nurse and traveling companion. In 1888, the Ings relocated to the Rural Health Retreat (later the St. Helena Sanitarium), where Jenny worked as the *matron.

inspiration. *See* revelation and inspiration.

intellect. The ability of the mind to think. "Human intellect is not omnipotent" (CE 37), yet God "can sharpen the intellect" (COL 146). The "great teachers" of the world, with "giant intellect and extensive research," are subservient before "One who stands higher than they. . . . Every gleam of thought, every flash of the intellect, is from the Light of the world" (Ed 13).

intercourse. A *Victorian term used to describe commerce, trade, or conversation. When Ellen G. White described the importance of having "intercourse with our heavenly Father," she meant that people should communicate with God as a friend (SC 93). Similarly, she noted how the ancient Israelites had intercourse (dialogue) with idolaters—the Edomites and other nations—who caused the Israelites to backslide (PP 363, 424, 435, 454). Similarly, Saul had intercourse with Satan through evil spirits (PP 638, 684). She also wrote of the "familiar intercourse [conversations] of the home circle" (AA 250) and how important it is that all "social intercourse" of a Christian should be "profitable" (DA 641).

irradiate. In the modern sense, *irradiate* typically refers to being exposed to radiation; but in antebellum America, it meant to illuminate something, often by shining a light on it. Ellen G. White wrote that the Old Testament is "irradiated with the glory of the Son of God" (DA 211).

Irwin, George A. (1844–1913). Minister and administrator. Irwin fought in the American Civil War; while imprisoned at the Confederates' Andersonville prison-of-war camp, he was converted. In 1885, he accepted the *Sabbath and soon afterward began denominational employment. He served as the president of the Ohio Conference (1889–1895), supervised the General Conference District no. 2 (the southern United States), and as the General Conference president (1897–1901). After the reorganization of the *church, Irwin served as a missionary to Australia, returned to serve as the vice president for North America (1909–1910), and as the president of the Pacific Union Conference (1910–1912).

Israel, modern. In Ellen G. White's first vision in December 1844, she described herself as someone who, like the biblical Caleb and Joshua, was sent to encourage people to *go forward to the heavenly Canaan land. Seventh-day Adventists should learn from the story of the ancient Israelites, especially from the curse of *Meroz, because God's people are indeed "His modern Israel" (2T 109; cf. 3T 396). Her allusions to *James White fulfilling a similar role to that of Moses was the basis for some of the earliest *criticism of their leadership by early dissidents, such as the *Marion Party.

J

Jackson, James Caleb (1811–1895). American health reformer. He founded the "water cure" establishment "Our Home on the Hillside" in Dansville, New York. Many early Seventh-day Adventist leaders, including James and Ellen G. White, sought medical treatment there. Although the Whites gleaned many natural remedies, Ellen G. White was particularly concerned about certain amusements and the lack of *exercise. She later contrasted some of the extreme practices of Jackson with those of the Seventh-day Adventists who developed their own views of healthful living.

Jones, Alonzo Treviér (1850–1923). Adventist minister. At the age of twenty, he joined the United States Army. He joined the Seventh-day Adventist Church in 1874; following his discharge from the army, he began *preaching in Washington and California. In May 1885, he became an assistant editor of *Signs of the Times*; and a short time later, he became a coeditor with *E. J. Waggoner. In 1887, he also became the editor of the **American Sentinel* and became widely recognized during the late 1880s and 1890s for his promulgation of religious liberty. At the *General Conference Session of 1888, he presented a *revival message about *justification by faith that Ellen G. White strongly supported. In 1901, he became caught up in a power struggle (along with Dr. *J. H. Kellogg) with *A. G. Daniells that led to his ultimate separation from the denomination.

joy. The gift of *salvation makes it possible for the Christian believer to experience joy and happiness. "There is nothing gloomy in the religion of Jesus" (MB 88).

justification by faith. An act of God's *grace to sinners that pardons all their sins and declares them righteous. This act is not based on merit but on the full *obedience of Jesus Christ, imputed to them by God and received by *faith alone. *See also* sanctification.

K

Kellogg, John Harvey (1852–1943). Physician, surgeon,

inventor, and author. Kellogg was born into *John Preston Kellogg's large family of seventeen children (although only nine survived to adulthood). James and Ellen G. White took an interest in J. H. Kellogg, who attended school with their own children. In 1873, the Whites urged him to attend R. T. Trall's Hygieo-Therapeutic College in New Jersey, and later he continued his education at the University of Michigan and the Bellevue Hospital Medical College. At the age of twenty-four, he was appointed as superintendent of the *Health Reform Institute. He later renamed it the *Battle Creek Sanitarium, and under his leadership, it became world renowned. Ellen G. White had a close relationship with Kellogg, and after his mother died, she thought of him as another son. After the 1901 General Conference Session, he became involved in a conflict with denominational leaders. Ellen G. White tried to arbitrate and admonished both Kellogg and the church leaders. Kellogg took the Battle Creek Sanitarium out of denominational ownership and was disfellowshiped in 1906. He afterward became an outspoken critic of Ellen G. White's prophetic ministry.

Kellogg, John Preston (1807–1881). Early Adventist from Michigan. Converted in 1852, Kellogg was part of a small group who pledged to build a publishing house in Battle Creek, Michigan, if *James White relocated from Rochester, New York. James White accepted the offer in 1855. He was a close friend of James and Ellen G. White and was a key financial supporter as the fledgling denomination developed.

Kellogg, Merritt Gardner (1832–1921). Minister, physician, and missionary. He was the oldest son of *John Preston Kellogg to survive childhood; at the age of twenty, he converted to Adventism. In 1859, he traveled to California by wagon to do missionary *work. In 1867, he attended

R. T. Trall's Hygieo-Therapeutic College in New Jersey. By 1870, he returned to California, was ordained in 1872, and in 1878 helped to found the Rural Health Retreat (the precursor to the St. Helena Sanitarium). In 1893, he traveled as a physician on board the **Pitcairn.* In his later years, he served as a medical missionary in Australia. He retired in 1903 in Healdsburg, California.

Kilgore, Robert Mead (1839–1912). Minister and administrator. In 1877, he traveled to Texas as a self-supporting evangelist. In 1885, he became the Illinois Conference president. At the *General Conference Session of 1888, Kilgore strongly resisted the *revival message brought by *A. T. Jones and *E. J. Waggoner. In his later years, he served in a variety of administrative posts, including leadership in the fledgling Graysville Academy (forerunner of Southern Adventist University).

kingdom of God. The rule or reign of God. Like many *Protestant Reformers, Ellen G. White highlighted that the kingdom of God was Christ's rule over the *church, not the rule of civil government. She believed that the kingdom of God would reign after the *Second Coming, when the redeemed will spend a millennium in heaven before the restoration of God's kingdom on the earth made new.

King, George Albert (1847–1906). Colporteur. Originally from Toronto, he converted in his twenties and by 1879 worked in Texas. He later served in a variety of places and suggested the idea of selling Uriah Smith's books *Thoughts, Critical and Practical, on the Book of Daniel* and *Thoughts, Critical and Practical, on the Book of Revelation* as an individual volume.

kingly power. An expression used by Ellen G. White, most often during the 1890s and early 1900s, to protest the controlling power of a single person, or small group of people, over the administration of the *church. She admonished in 1901 that "God has not put any kingly power in our ranks to control this or that branch of the work. The work has been greatly restricted by the efforts to control it in every line" (GCB Apr. 3, 1901).

king's dale. A biblical location mentioned in Genesis 14:17 and 2 Samuel 18:18 that describes the "king's dale," or the "king's vale," as the name for "the valley of Shaveh" where the king of Sodom met Abram and where Absalom built a monument for himself (PP 744).

Kinney, Charles M. (1855–1951). Early black minister. Born a slave in Richmond, Virginia, he worked in Reno, Nevada, as a youth. While there, in 1878, he attended a series of meetings held by *J. N. Loughborough, which included a lecture by Ellen G. White, and was subsequently baptized. He attended *Healdsburg College from 1883 to 1885, pastored in Topeka, Kansas, and by 1889 worked with black believers in St. Louis, Missouri. Kinney played an instrumental role in the development of the *work for black Americans. He organized several of the earliest black Adventist congregations and is considered the founder of black Adventism.

Knight, Anna (1874–1972). Leading black Seventh-day Adventist missionary and educator. She taught herself to read and obtained a *Bible by picking cotton. She was baptized in 1893 and studied nursing under Dr. *J. H. Kellogg. At the 1901 General Conference Session, she was sent as a missionary to India (the first black Adventist woman to do so). She later established a church and a school in Mississippi and served in a variety of posts in conjunction with Adventist *education.

knowledge of God. The intellectual and experiential awareness of God. Ellen G. White believed, like many during the *Protestant Reformation, that there was a common distinction between a natural knowledge of God obtained through *general revelation and a saving knowledge of God received through *special revelation.

L

Laodicea. A term based upon the biblical *church in Asia Minor and referred to in Revelation. This church was in a lukewarm state. Beginning in 1856, Ellen G. White applied the message for the Laodicean church to God's *remnant people.

lassitude. A state of weariness or lack of energy (3T 11; 4T 96; MH 292).

latter rain. The latter rain was the final refreshing moisture that crops in the Middle East needed to finish maturation. Similar to the *early rain, Ellen G. White pointed to the final work of the *Holy Spirit in preparing God's *remnant people immediately before the *Second Advent. "The latter rain, ripening earth's harvest, represents the spiritual grace that prepares the church for the coming of the Son of man" (TM 506). *See also* revival.

law of God. Ellen White understood the "law of God" first as the moral law contained in the Decalogue of Exodus 20: 3–17, and secondly as the natural laws as found in nature. Ellen G. White described the laws of God and the laws of *nature as complementary; thus, they shed *light upon each other (Ed 128). Natural law is under the "continual and direct agency of God" (8T 259). There is no dichotomy between the two because "the laws of nature are the laws of God" (Ed 196). "To transgress His [God's] law, physical, mental, or moral, is to place one's self out of harmony with the universe" (Ed 100). Unfortunately, the natural world appears contradictory at times due to the fact that it is marred by sin, leaving the *Bible as the one sure guide to discover *truth (Ed 134).

Lay, Horatio S. (1828–1900). Physician and founding director of the *Health Reform Institute. Lay attended Western Reserve College in Hudson, Ohio, and earned a medical degree from the Detroit Medical College. He practiced medicine in Allegan, Michigan, and in 1856 accepted the *Sabbath. In 1862, after his wife Julia (1831–1893) suffered poor health, he brought her to *James C. Jackson's water-cure establishment to receive treatment. He joined the staff of "Our Home on the Hillside" until 1866, when he returned to Allegan. He then founded the Health Reform Institute and started the first Adventist health periodical, the *Health Reformer*.

lazar house. A leper colony; known today as a quarantine area for those who suffer from Hansen's disease. Ellen G. White described the whole world as a "vast lazar house" in need of the message of salvation (DA 823; cf. 4T 30).

lees. A term that refers to the dead yeast in wine that settles to the bottom during aging. Ellen G. White used the term to describe someone who is lazy: "reclining on their lees" (Zephaniah 1:12, KJV) (5T 203).

liberality. A term used to indicate generosity. Ellen G. White used the term, for example, to refer to the believers in Corinth (AA 335–337). "The spirit of liberality is the spirit of heaven" (4T 79).

lifestyle, Adventist. *Adventist lifestyle* is a term that describes how Adventists live their everyday lives—including their diet, dress, and even their recreational activities. "He who would serve Christ cannot follow the world's opinions or meet the world's standard" (MB 139). The Adventist lifestyle includes learning principles and then applying them. "When Christ abides in the heart, there will be purity and refinement of thought and manner" (MB 25).

light. A visual term and theological motif that appears throughout Ellen G. White's writings. In her first vision, she describes Jesus Christ as the source of light to God's people who are on a straight and narrow path. She contrasts this light with darkness. Those who took their eyes from Jesus fell off the path (LS 64, 65). Darkness is simply the absence of light. Progressive truth is light that illumines both heart and mind. As a person comprehends *truth, his mind expands as "pure streams of light pour into his soul" (4T 414). Christians thus become "channels of God's light" to others (4T 80). They are accountable to God for the light they have received, lest it become darkness (2T 123), and they must feel their need for additional light before more light will come (4T 611).

lineament(s). A distinctive feature or characteristic (DA 804).

listlessness. Lack of inclination or impetus to exert oneself (PP 729).

Litch, Josiah (1809–1886). Millerite revivalist and author. Originally a *Methodist Episcopal minister, he first read the writings of *William Miller in 1838. Initially hostile, he adopted the *Second Advent message. In his book *The Probability of the Second Coming of Christ About A.D. 1843*, he predicted that the Ottoman Empire would lose power in August of 1840. When the Ottoman Empire accepted the guarantees of the Great Powers of Europe, which Litch believed went into effect on August 11, 1840, this was widely accepted as a fulfillment of Bible prophecy. Litch shared his faith with *Charles Fitch. After the *Great Disappointment, he participated in the 1845 Albany Conference that opposed other Adventists who believed in visions and the seventh-day *Sabbath. He later became a prominent part of the evangelical Adventists, formed his own organization called Messianians, and ultimately abandoned his historicist views of prophecy.

living epistle(s). A *living epistle* is when Christ is revealed in one's daily life (4T 376). The example of a living epistle is therefore a powerful testimony of God's power to change lives.

Loma Linda University. See College of Medical Evangelists.

Lord's Supper (also Communion). The sharing and partaking of bread and wine that symbolizes the broken body and blood of Jesus Christ. During the 1840s, Ellen G. White cautioned against certain *fanatics, especially men who wished to wash the feet of women, but retained the practice of Communion within early Adventism. With time, she articulated an "Adventist understanding" of the rite that emphasized the death of Christ (the First Advent) and the affirmation of their belief in Christ's soon return.

Loughborough, John Norton (1832–1924). Minister, missionary, and administrator. He wrote the first denominational history, *The Rise and Progress of Seventh-day Adventists* (1892), which was later revised and enlarged as *The Great Second Advent Movement* (1905). In 1868, he and *D. T. Bourdeau traveled as missionaries to California and in 1878 moved to England for five years. Loughborough held a wide variety of administrative posts in the denomination and was a close friend of James and Ellen G. White.

love. Ellen G. White spoke repeatedly and consistently throughout her lifetime about God's love, which is revealed through the outworking of the plan of salvation. During her lifetime, she contrasted it with the view that love is God's chief attribute and she warned of downgrading it "to a weak sentimentalism, making little distinction between good and evil" (GC 558). "If the love of Jesus does not subdue the heart, there are no means by which we can be reached" (COL 237). *See also* lovesick sentimentalism.

lovesick sentimentalism. A phrase commonly used (in conjunction with educational schools) to describe infatuated boys and girls who are enamored with one another (2T 482). Typically, Ellen G. White admonished against such *attachments because of the inability of young people to make objective decisions and recognize the lifelong commitment that *marriage entails.

lung fever. A very ambiguous medical term, sometimes used to refer to pneumonia (HR Apr. 1, 1871).

Luther, Martin (1483–1546). Ellen G. White described Martin Luther, in contrast with other famous leaders in world history, as an example of someone who, despite his humble birth, "stood bravely for truth and right" (4T 519). Ellen G. White wrote more about Luther than about any other religious Reformer in her book *The Great Controversy*. She extolled his example as one that will encourage God's *remnant people at the end of time to stand for Bible *truth (GC 607, 609).

M

Magan, Percy Tilson (1867–1947). Physician and administrator. Born in Ireland, he became an Adventist in Red Cloud, Nebraska, in 1886. He initially worked as a colporteur and then in 1887 received a license to preach. In 1889, he worked as a secretary to *S. N. Haskell while they were on a world missionary tour. He served as an associate secretary of the Foreign Mission Board (1890–1891) and taught Bible and history at *Battle Creek College (1891–1901). About 1899, he partnered with *E. A. Sutherland to relocate Battle Creek College to a more rural location, which occurred two years later when the school moved to Berrien Springs, Michigan. This move allowed him to implement educational reforms. After 1904, he worked with Sutherland to found Madison College, a self-supporting school, to continue their educational reforms. He earned an MD degree from the University of Tennessee (1910–1914) and later became the dean (1915–1928) and the president (1928–1940) of the *College of Medical Evangelists (later Loma Linda University).

magnanimity. A greatness of mind, including the elevation or dignity of the soul when encountering danger and trouble. Such behavior prompts personal sacrifice and disdains unjustness and meanness (PP 660).

malignant. This term can mean evil, dangerous, or harmful, such as a malignant growth or "humor" (tumor). In the spiritual sense, Ellen G. White warned, "Today sin is the same malignant thing that it was in the time of Adam" (FW 96).

mammon. A term used to describe worldliness and, frequently, the love of money (2T 237–247). While Ellen G. White used the word in a variety of associations, she wrote that it was the fatal flaw of Judas, the disciple of Jesus Christ (DA 716).

manacled. In chains or bonds. Ellen G. White described the apostle Paul who was "manacled" (AA 434, 438).

Manassas, Battle of First. The first major battle of the Civil War occurred near Manassas, Virginia, on July 21, 1861; it is also called the First Battle of Bull Run. It was considered a *Confederate victory because around four o'clock that afternoon the entire Union army collapsed and retreated back to Washington, D.C. Both sides expected Manassas to be the decisive battle that would end the war, but they were shocked at the bloody aftermath. On August 3, about two weeks later, Ellen G. White had a vision about the "disastrous battle at Manassas" and saw an angel descend at a crucial moment in the battle. The angel, she said, caused "confusion in the ranks" of the advancing Northern forces and "a precipitate [sudden] retreat commenced." The outcome of the *North's loss was that God still "had this nation in His own hand, and would not suffer victories to be gained faster than He ordained, and would permit no more losses to the Northern men than in His wisdom He saw fit, to punish them for their sins [of tolerating slavery in the South]" (1T 266, 267).

maniac. A mentally ill person. Ellen G. White warned

about those who suffer from addictions, including the maniac, who need to be educated about the results of breaking health laws (MH 114).

manliness. A *Victorian movement that emphasized the role of men in the private and public spheres. Ellen G. White appealed for a biblical view of manliness and that husbands and fathers had a significant role to play within the *home circle. She said those men who practice *temperance by avoiding "wine, beer, and strong drinks" show "true manliness" (CTBH 37). *See also* womanliness.

Marion Party. An offshoot group based in Marion, Iowa, during the 1860s that was led by B. F. Snook and W. H. Brinkerhoff. They defected over Ellen G. White's prophetic leadership. The group became the forerunner of the Church of God (Seventh Day), with offices today in Denver, Colorado. Snook and Brinkerhoff were agitated over the issue of pacifism versus conscientious cooperation and combatantcy. Since James and Ellen G. White did not strongly support strict pacifism, these men began to believe that Ellen G. White could not be a true prophet. Snook and Brinkerhoff developed a critical spirit in response to the messages of *reproof they received at the 1865 Iowa Conference meeting. Despite their confessions, they were not given back their positions of responsibility. *G. I. Butler replaced Snook as the conference president. Over the following years, their doubts resumed, which resulted in their permanent estrangement from the Whites and the Seventh-day Adventist Church.

mark of the beast. The sign of the worshipers of the first beast in Revelation 13, which is generally understood by most *Protestant interpreters as the Roman Catholic

Church. Early Sabbatarian Adventists, most notably *J. N. Andrews and *James White, adopted this position and correlated Sunday observance as the distinguishing mark of this papal institution. Ellen G. White, in her most extensive treatment on the subject (the chapter "God's Law Immutable" in *The Great Controversy*), identified this mark as the counterfeit to the seal of God. "What then is the change of the Sabbath, but the sign, or mark, of the authority of the Roman Church—'the mark of the beast'?" (GC 448).

marriage. A sacred covenant between a man and a woman that was instituted in the Garden of Eden by God. Marriage does not destroy the individuality of the person (2T 100). Ellen G. White noted that although "marriage has been perverted by sin," part of the work of the gospel is to restore "its purity and beauty." "The grace of Christ" alone "can make this institution what God designed it should be—an agent for the blessing and uplifting of humanity" (MB 64, 65).

matron. A person in charge of a college's dining room, health restaurant, nursing department, or the food service in a school or sanitarium. Ellen G. White counseled that a sanitarium should hire a "competent" matron and the employees should *work faithfully and be paid "just wages" (CH 314).

Matteson, John Gottlieb (1835–1896). Minister, missionary, and author. Originally from Denmark, Matteson immigrated to the United States, where he accepted the Adventist message. From 1877 to 1888, he served as a missionary to Scandinavia; he was also the personal guide and translator for Ellen G. White during her missionary tour through Europe (1885–1887). He founded the first non-English Adventist periodical, *Advent Tidende*; translated Ellen G.

White's books; and founded a publishing house in Norway.

means. A reference to money or resources. Ellen G. White often connected the word *means* with "advancing the work of the gospel" (AA 71).

meditate/meditation. Ellen G. White frequently encouraged people to spend time in daily *prayer, Bible study, and meditation, with a heart longing after God. Meditation consists of "emptying and purifying the heart, and must be nurtured by daily prayer" (4T 535). It is taking a verse of Scripture and concentrating "the mind on the task of ascertaining the thought which God has put in that verse for us. We should dwell upon the thought until it becomes our own, and we know 'what saith the Lord' " (DA 390). Unlike other forms of meditation that merely emptied the mind, she noted that biblical meditation was something that filled the mind with *truth. She encouraged, for example, people to meditate upon the words of Christ and not to merely repeat them "parrot-like"—referring to a parrot that mindlessly mimics other creatures (4T 355). Meditation was a time to listen for the personal word of God to one's soul: "We must individually hear Him speaking to the heart. When every other voice is hushed, . . . the silence of the soul makes more distinct the voice of God" (DA 363).

mental culture. The "pursuit of knowledge" that leads to "clearer and brighter views of the wonderful laws of science and of nature" (4T 414). Ellen G. White argued that "mental culture," or the "cultivation of the mind," was essential for all church members to have "in order to meet the demands of the time" (4T 414). "All intellectual laziness is sin," she counseled (4T 399). Thus, the need for mental culture is why Adventist *education is so important.

Meroz. A common term in the nineteenth century that referred to the story of the city of Meroz. During the Israelite sojourn in the wilderness, the inhabitants of Meroz sinned by doing nothing (2T 395, 427, 550, 626; 3T 525). "We are responsible," wrote Ellen G. White, "for the good we might have done, but failed to do because we were too indolent to use the means for improvement which were placed within our reach" (4T 416).

mesmerism. The practice of inducing a hypnotic trance, popularized by Franz Anton Mesmer (1734–1815), an Austrian physician. Others later built on Mesmer's ideas of *animal magnetism and developed the practice of inducing a deep trance by staring intensely into the eyes of the patient and passing the hand over the head and around the body (sometimes with a magnet). This induced trance state was eventually called mesmerism—known today as hypnotism. Mesmerism was introduced in America during the late 1820s and spread across the East Coast, especially in the big cities such as Boston and New York. By the early 1840s, lectures and public demonstrations of magnetism were immensely popular. The young Ellen White encountered mesmerists during the mid-1840s and considered any form of mind control to be a form of spiritualism (EW 21, 108, 109; 1T 71).

Methodist/Methodism. Denomination arising from the teachings of *John Wesley in the eighteenth century; its adherents are known as Methodists, initially a pejorative term. Ellen G. White was raised in the Chestnut Street Methodist Church in Portland, Maine, and was baptized on June 26, 1842, by the Reverend John Hobart. The majority of early Sabbatarian Adventist ministers were previously ordained as Methodist ministers, so Methodism had a significant influence, among others—such as the Baptists and Christian Connexion—that contributed to early Adventist discussions, such as vocabulary, structure, and the articulation of beliefs.

miasma. Before the germ theory of disease, most people believed that the *air contained *miasma*, or harmful properties that caused illness. The term was a catchall phrase to describe anything dirty or potentially harmful (PP 44). At times, Ellen G. White referred to it as a spiritual pollutant, such as the "miasma of jealousy" (DA 179).

mien. A person's outward look indicating one's *character or mood. Ellen G. White described some biblical characters as having a "noble mien" (PP 729) or a "dignified mien" (DA 223).

millennialism. The *doctrine of the millennium, or the thousand-year time period after the *Second Coming. During the early nineteenth century, most Protestant Christians believed in the post-millennium—the idea that the *Second Advent would occur after the millennium. William Miller as part of the Millerite revival argued that the Second Advent would instead occur before the millennium (premillennialism). At the end of the millennium, there will still be a final judgment, which includes the final eradication of sin when Satan and his followers are destroyed and the earth is made new.

Millerite revival. From the 1830s through the 1840s, the Millerite revival was a large-scale revival that most conservative historians estimate had from fifty thousand to one hundred thousand adherents. Founded by Baptist farmer *William Miller after he shared his views about Bible prophecy, the movement quickly grew under the leadership of *Joshua V. Himes and the *preaching of itinerant ministers such as *Josiah Litch and *Charles Fitch.

Miller, William (1782–1849). Farmer and revivalist. As a young person, William Miller was a prodigious reader and imbibed deistic and democratic notions. With upward social mobility, he obtained increasingly visible positions in the community, becoming a surveyor of roads and a justice of the peace. During the War of 1812, he served as a captain in the army and led his men through the Battle of Plattsburgh. In 1816, he experienced a *conversion that led to the systematic study of the *Bible. By 1818, he concluded from his reading of Daniel 8:14 that Christ would return around 1843. Initially reluctant to share his findings, he ultimately became the leading advocate in the United States and Canada of the *second coming of Christ. He was also the namesake for a religious *revival that occurred as part of the Second Great Awakening in antebellum America. After the *Great Disappointment, he clung to his faith in the soon return of Christ until his death in 1849.

minutemen. People who can stand faithful in the midst of battle on short notice. The term has a historical reference to militia troops during the American Revolution; but by the time of Ellen G. White, it was a general expression to refer to the need for help (PP 423).

missiles. Throwing projectiles of some kind, such as rocks (PP 390).

mission. Mission is an essential part of the Christian message in which followers of Jesus Christ share their faith, or witness to others. Adventists were initially hesitant to embrace mission. Early Sabbatarian Adventists believed in the "*shut door," which is the view that, in essence, the door of *probation closed after October 22, 1844. During the late 1840s and early 1850s, this became a partially open door. The emergence of missions occurred during the 1860s as the penultimate major organizational development (followed by Adventist *education in 1874). After *church organization in 1863, the *church was ready to send out missionaries. One of the earliest attempts was by *M. B. Czechowski, who did not receive official support, so he solicited the Advent Christian Church to send him as a missionary. The first significant attempt was by *J. N. Loughborough and *D. T. Bourdeau in 1868. The following year James Ertzenberger came to Battle Creek, Michigan, to obtain training and then returned to Europe in 1870 as an ordained minister. He was the first overseas missionary with the specific intent of returning to share the Advent message in Europe. As mission service expanded, so did missionary consciousness. In 1874, *J. N. Andrews and his children, Mary and Charles, were sent officially as the denomination's first American-born missionaries. During the 1880s and 1890s, mission outposts expanded to Australia, Africa, and South America. In 1896, Ellen G. White wrote that Christ "has committed to His followers a world-wide mission" (MB 42). The golden age of Adventist missions occurred during the 1920s as these early efforts expanded to most countries around the world. Adventist missions changed after the Global Mission initiative of 1990 when Adventists recognized the large number of unentered population segments around the globe.

modern Israel. *See* Israel, modern.

monomaniac. A term used to describe a *one-idea man who

is crazy. "We see monomaniacs all over the country. They are frequently sane upon every subject but one" (3T 33).

moral courage (also moral fitness/power/worth). The term *moral courage* had a rich meaning in connection with *Victorian *moral philosophy that stressed the importance of moral conduct, both private and public. Ellen G. White used the term in connection with the Spirit of God, who enables a person to be able to renounce hurtful *habits (3T 194; 4T 32, 431). Such a person is obtaining a "moral fitness for heaven" (3T 575). Such *work is spiritual warfare (4T 36). Those who stumble fall into "moral darkness"; but if they have "moral stamina," they can create a "moral atmosphere" (4T 172, 184, 206). In another instance, she described a man whose friends criticized him, causing a "moral shock" to him both "spiritually and physically" (4T 327).

moral government of God. The justice and fairness of God's rule across the universe. Ellen G. White was strongly influenced by the ideas of John Milton and early Anabaptists on the moral government of God. These concepts were developed by Hugo Grotius (1583–1645), who wrote the first book of modern apologetics. Ellen G. White was especially impacted by these thoughts as presented through *Methodism and the commentaries of Albert Barnes (1798–1870). It was this theological framework that laid the foundation for her ideas about the *great controversy conflict between Christ and Satan.

moral philosophy. A term equivalent to ethics, which "teaches men their duty and the reasons of it."(Noah Webster, *American Dictionary of the English Languarge*, 1828) Historians often refer to it in a broad sense as "natural philosophy," which during the nineteenth century included a broad study of anything as concerning right and wrong, *nature, and the rational study of meaning and the justification of moral claims. Together these revealed truths tell about humanity and human relationships. Ellen G. White included the study of "moral philosophy, the study of the Scriptures, and physical training" as essential for *education (CE 210).

More, Hannah (1808–1868). Missionary and early convert to Adventism (1866). A veteran missionary and educator, she was treated with derision by believers in Battle Creek, Michigan, which brought forth a strong message of rebuke from Ellen G. White (1T 666–679; 2T 140–144). She stayed with a missionary family in northwest Michigan during the winter of 1867 and 1868. James and Ellen G. White promised to help her relocate to Battle Creek after the winter, but she grew ill and died. Ellen G. White strongly condemned the harsh treatment by church members.

murrain. A nineteenth-century term for infectious diseases and *death (PP 267).

music. The Millerites and early Sabbatarian Adventists published a number of hymns that reflected their belief in the *second advent of Christ. Many early tunes were adapted from popular music of the period. Adventist musicians such as *F. E. Belden composed unique musical pieces as Seventh-day Adventists developed their own unique music with their own unique theological concepts and liturgical practices.

N

national fasts. *Puritan ritual of turning to God. During the American Civil War, the fasts were held particularly to ask for the war to end. Ellen G. White warned that such fasts would do no good (1T 257–259). Early Adventists participated in fasts of their own as the question of military service and a national draft severely drained financial resources in the fledgling denomination.

natural philosophy. *See* moral philosophy.

nature. The physical world is the great lesson book to learn about the Creator (Ed 99–101). "Nature still speaks to us of God's goodness" (Ed 101). Unfortunately, due to sin, "only in the light that shines from Calvary can nature's teaching be read aright" (Ed 101). "There are wonderful truths in nature. . . . Sin has obscured his [humanity's] vision," Ellen G. White noted, "and he cannot of himself interpret nature without placing it above God" (COL 107).

necromancy. The practice of revealing future events by attempting to communicate with the dead. Ellen G. White described how evil spirits were at work with King Saul and the witch of Endor (PP 676).

nicest work. A superlative term used by Ellen G. White to describe the *detail* required of Adventist educators (3T 131, 269). The *work of the Adventist educator is a solemn responsibility and requires great care and tact to help mold minds and aid students in developing characters for heaven.

niggardly. Being ungenerous with one's money or time (2T 284; 4T 126). Ellen G. White described the selfish behavior of Nabal in his treatment of David and his men as "churlish and niggardly" (PP 664).

night season. A reference to nighttime. Ellen G. White

often associated this term in reference to supernatural instruction she received while she slept. For example, "the word of the Lord came to me in the night season" (CS 264). Biblical figures such as Balaam received divine instruction at nighttime (PP 440). Biblical prophets could receive divine instruction either during the day or at night.

North. A reference, particularly during the American Civil War (1861–1865), to the states that supported the Union. In the United States presidential election of 1860, the Republican Party dominated the North, the states north of the Mason-Dixon line, and won a plurality of the popular votes and a majority of the electoral votes nationally. This secured the election of Abraham Lincoln (1809–1865) as president. In response, eleven states in the *South seceded, which forced a confrontation that resulted in the bloodiest war in United States history. Ellen G. White expressed caution about the reluctance of *proslavery men in the North to stand up against slavery (1T 253–268).

nostrums. Ellen G. White warned against many popular and patent nostrums, or medicines, that were positively unhealthful and even dangerous. She advised health reformers instead to make use of natural remedies. Some of these nostrums contained harmful substances that led to alcohol, opium, or morphine addictions that were a "terrible a curse upon society" (MH 126, 127).

O

Oakwood Industrial School. A boarding school begun for black Americans on November 16, 1896. The school was begun largely through the urging of Ellen G. White, who saw in a night vision that a school should be begun in

Huntsville, Alabama (see Lt. 25, 1902, in 2MR 64). Now known as Oakwood University.

obedience. Compliance with a request, order, or law. Ellen G. White described the *law of God as timeless and unchanging. It existed before the world was made and, through the example of Jesus while on this earth, is a "perpetual obligation" (MB 48). Jesus came "to give an example of perfect conformity to the will of God" (MB 49). "Christ testified to its immutable character and proved that through His grace it could be perfectly obeyed by every son and daughter of Adam" (MB 49). Ellen G. White also noted that "true obedience is the outworking of a principle within. It springs from the love of righteousness" (COL 97). "Good works do not purchase the love of God," she noted, "but they reveal that we possess that love" (COL 283).

office. A term typically used to refer to the Review and Herald office—the main publishing house in Battle Creek, Michigan, which was relocated to Takoma Park, Maryland, in 1903.

Olsen, Ole Andres (1845–1915). Minister and administrator. Originally from Skogan, Norway, he immigrated to Wisconsin in 1850. He accepted the Adventist message in 1854. He began ministerial work in Wisconsin in 1869 among Scandinavian immigrants. Ordained in 1873, he served as the conference president in Wisconsin (1874–1876; 1880–1881), Dakota (1882–1883), Minnesota (1883–1885), and Iowa (1884–1885). In 1886, he served as a missionary to Scandinavia. After the tumultuous *General Conference Session of 1888, Olsen was elected as church president because he was perceived as a spiritual and capable leader as well as a neutral person in the conflict.

He was slow to make decisions, which brought him into further conflict. Beginning in 1897, he worked in South Africa, Europe, and Australia; in 1909 as the secretary of the North American Foreign Department; and as the vice president of the North American Division in 1913.

one-idea man. An expression used by Ellen G. White to describe certain individuals who had one-track minds (3T 34). They emphasized one idea to the exclusion of everything else. Such individuals were *fanatics.

opprobrious. An adjective expressing scorn or *criticism. Ellen G. White described the opposition Millerites faced by stating that *William Miller himself was subject to "opprobrious epithets" for his belief in the *Second Advent (GC 336).

ordination. The formal recognition of ministry by the laying on of hands. Early Adventist ministers primarily came from *Methodist and Baptist backgrounds. During the 1850s, some ministers were rebaptized and reordained. During the 1860s and 1870s, young ministers were ordained to the ministry as a recognition of God's calling. These early services largely reflected *Protestant ordination services that merely recognized God's call and did not confer any special privilege or status.

organization, church. Early church leaders were suspicious of any and all forms of organization. During the *Millerite revival, some argued that any steps toward organization led to Babylon. Thus, early Sabbatarian Adventists strongly resisted attempts to organize. Yet pragmatic considerations, largely driven by the need to own and operate a press along with church publications, and mounting financial obligations led to repeated appeals to consider the possibility of organization. Further challenges, brought about by the need to properly register churches under a legal name, arose as the children of some believers closed churches after the death of their parents. All of this came to a head when the *church formally adopted the name *Seventh-day Adventist* in 1860, created the first association of churches as a state *conference in 1861, and formally organized as the General Conference in 1863. This structure was significantly reorganized at the 1901 General Conference Session. Various church entities were unified by creating various departments in the denomination. Conferences were consolidated into "unions" of conferences. In 1913 and 1918, these union conferences were merged into "divisions" of the General Conference. Thus, church organization today is reflected in five levels of church hierarchy: (1) local church, (2) conference, (3) union conference, (4) division, and (5) General Conference.

overcome/overcomer. The Christian has a responsibility through the *grace of Jesus Christ to develop a *character that reflects Jesus and prepares the person to live a better life both now and in the world to come. In her *testimonies she frequently appealed for people to become overcomers. "Through the impacted grace of Christ," she wrote, each believer "may be enabled to overcome. To be an overcomer means more than many suppose it means" (1SM 380).

overreach/overreaching. The tendency of some people to extend beyond their own responsibilities. For example, Ellen G. White talked about church members who pry into the business of others or who have a *faultfinding spirit. Such individuals should not overreach but should concern themselves with their own spiritual growth. She furthermore warned against "overreaching in trade" so that Christians in all of their business dealings are fair and honest (PP 309).

P

Palmer, Edwin R. (1869–1931). Colporteur and publishing house manager. Born in Vermont, he attended the South Lancaster Academy in Massachusetts. He married Eva Maynard in 1893 and sold literature in Vermont, Oklahoma, and Australia. From 1901 to 1902, he served as the general agent of literature work for the world field and from 1907 to 1912 as the secretary of the Publishing Department of the General Conference. He was the general manager of the Review and Herald Publishing Association from 1912 to 1931. He also served as the principal of Avondale College (1899–1901) and as the manager of the Paradise Valley Sanitarium in California (1904–1905).

panoply. A term used in the title of the book *The Divine Panoply* by J. Walker, which was published in 1846. The term, as evinced in the second title of the book, refers to *A Suit of Armour for the Soldier of Christ.* While the book is not registered in the extant bibliography of Ellen G. White's personal and office library, her usages of the phrase suggest that she was familiar with this particular volume. She therefore talks about being clothed "with the panoply of God" (DA 779), "with a divine panoply" (DA 353), "in the panoply of truth" (AA 495), or "with the panoply of heaven" (AA 220).

pantheism. The idea that a force or power encompasses all of the universe (or *nature). *Pantheism* is the belief that God is greater than the universe but interpenetrates parts of it—namely animated beings. Ellen G. White used the term *pantheism* loosely while warning against the teachings of Dr. *J. H. Kellogg (which really were *panentheistic*), which she viewed as a serious threat to *Seventh-day Adventist theology (5BIO 287–289).

P

paramour. A lover, especially an illicit partner of a married person. Ellen G. White described Herodias, the wife of Herod's brother, as the "vile paramour" (DA 215).

parenting. Ellen G. White was the mother of four boys and wrote extensively about parenting. She told parents that they must "labor intelligently" for the *conversion of their children. She contrasted parents who do not *discipline their children, such as the biblical Eli, with other parents who carry *reproof too far, "especially when vital godliness is not exemplified in the life of those who administer the reproof" (4T 609).

parley. A conference between opposing sides in a dispute. Ellen G. White often used the term to describe how Christians should not "parley with temptation" (DA 120).

paroxysm. A convulsion; also an outburst. It derives from a Greek word that means to excite or sharpen. It was used in antebellum America to describe the intensification of a disease or a fever that could intermittently come and go (PP 650).

"passing of the time." A phrase used by Ellen G. White to refer to the *Great Disappointment when Jesus Christ did not return as expected by faithful Millerites. As a young girl, Ellen had heard *William Miller preach, and, like many other Millerites, considered the year leading up to the great day of anticipation as "the happiest year of my life" (CET 51). When Christ did not return, like many others, she was deeply disappointed.

passions. This word is most often used by Ellen G. White in the phrase "fiery passions" to describe an individual's *temper or someone who becomes emotional (4T 367). She also warned against *animal propensities by indulging in the "lower passions" (PP 378).

patent nostrums. *See* nostrums.

pattern of Christ. Although this phrase is used only nine times in Ellen G. White's published writings, variations on this idea were used several hundred times. Every Christian should model his or her life upon the "pattern of Christ" (HR Nov. 1, 1878).

pauper/pauperism. A person who is very poor and often unemployed and/or homeless. Ellen G. White wrote an entire chapter in *The Ministry of Healing* about the need to help such individuals (183–200).

Peck, Sarah Elizabeth (1868–1968). Educator, missionary, and author. Beginning in 1898, she served as a literary assistant to Ellen G. White in Australia, where she organized a new filing system and worked as a bookkeeper. She helped to compile *Testimonies for the Church*, volume 6 (1900) and *Education* (1903). After 1903, Peck served as a teacher at a nearby church school. She contributed her skills to the *True Education Readers* series and other denominational textbooks.

peevish. Easily irritated by unimportant things. "Fretful and peevish fathers and mothers are giving their children lessons which at some period in their lives they would give all the world, were it theirs, could they unlearn" (AH 322).

penury. Extreme poverty or destitution (GC 20).

P

perfection. Ellen G. White used the terms "perfection," "sanctification," and "holiness" interchangeably throughout her writings to describe the process of the believer's character transformation into the likeness of Christ. Her use of the term "perfection" never conveyed a point of sinless perfection that Christians attain. "So long as Satan reigns, we shall have self to subdue, besetting sins to overcome; so long as life shall last, there will be no stopping place, no point which we can reach and say, I have fully attained." (AA 560–561). Rather, she described "perfection of Christian character" as an ongoing, lifelong process that involves continual advancement: "Every day we may advance in perfection of Christian character" (MH 503). Her view of perfection embraced several levels of Christian experience: (1) reckoned perfection when the believer is accounted as legally perfect through justification; (2) relative perfection when the believer is relatively perfect through ongoing sanctification and victory over known sin; (3) "time of trouble" perfection when believers would rather die than knowingly sin; (4) sinless perfection at glorification that is achieved only at the Second Coming when the saints receive immortality (see Woodrow W. Whidden, "Perfection," in the *Ellen G. White Encyclopedia*, 1021–1024).

perfidy. Deceitfulness or untrustworthiness. Ellen G. White used this term as a characteristic of the priests who opposed Jesus (DA 722, 727).

persecution. The use of force, whether coercive or willful, to pressure people to do something against their will. "In all ages Satan has persecuted the people of God" (MB 30). Ellen G. White states that "the character of the persecution changes with the times" (MB 29).

perspicuity of Scripture. The *doctrine of the clarity of Scripture is a *Protestant Reformation notion that is closely aligned with *sola scriptura*, or the *Bible alone. This *Protestant doctrine differs with the Roman Catholic Church teaching that Scripture is imperspicuous (unclear) apart from its interpretation through the *church and tradition. Early Seventh-day Adventists were influenced by the restorationist movement, which emphasized a return to the early New Testament church, including the priesthood of all believers. Thus, early Adventists believed that an ordinary person is capable of comprehending God's will through Scripture. Ellen G. White emphasized that through the *Holy Spirit the "vital truths" of salvation are "made so plain that none need err therein" (COL 113).

pestilential. Prone to plagues or infectious diseases. Ellen G. White noted the need for people to go to "the dark places of the earth" to proclaim the gospel, which requires sacrifice. In contrast, some people for "worldly advantage" are "willing to venture into pestilential regions" (PK 173).

pet/petting. Ellen G. White used this term to describe how parents indulge, or "pet," their children. Such parents tend to be lax and avoid disciplining their children. Occasionally, this term was used to portray individuals who show favoritism by "petting" others or church members who indulge, or "pet," their pastors by inflating their egos through praising their sermons.

petulant/petulance. Bad tempered or childish. Ellen G. White described certain individuals as being petulant (4T 129, 347; MH 219) and, in one instance, how people have prayed petulant *prayers (OHC 147).

philanthropy. *See* stewardship.

Phillips (Rice), Anna (1865–1926). Visionary, who for a brief time, claimed to have the prophetic gift. In 1892, Anna began to receive visions but was unable to obtain guidance from Ellen G. White. She counseled with *A. T. Jones instead. He believed in and strongly promulgated her prophetic gift through February 1894. Ellen G. White warned that such visions should not be endorsed "without sufficient evidence" (2SM 92). She did not blame Anna but, instead, rebuked those who promoted her in these visions. Jones and *W. W. Prescott expressed regret for their role, and Anna repudiated her claims. She later served the denomination as a Bible worker.

phrenology. A precursor to modern psychiatry and modern neuroscience that examined the physical contours of the skull to determine various physical and moral characteristics. It was common for patients to have their heads read when admitted to a medical institution.

phthisic. A *Victorian term referring to a wasting disease, particularly of the lungs (2T 349).

physiognomy. A phrenological term that is derived from the Greek words *physis* meaning "nature" and *gnōmōn* meaning to "judge" or "interpret." Thus, *physiognomy* refers to ascertaining information from the physical characteristics of a person.

picnic. A term used to describe a fashionable and public entertainment in which people contributed food to a common table. In Ellen G. White's time, large July 4th (American Independence Day) holiday picnics resembled a circus or fair. A Fourth of July picnic she attended in 1882 was characterized by a modest meal and thanksgiving to God, *prayer, and singing (3BIO 201). The term could also mean a *family or church gathering for outdoor recreation.

piety. For Ellen G. White, *piety* meant a daily, "consecrated life" to God that was not "outward forms" (4T 609).

Pitcairn. Missionary ship. As early as 1876, *James White and *J. N. Loughborough sent a box of literature to Pitcairn Island. Ten years later *John I. Tay (1832–1892) traveled to Pitcairn and, after Bible studies and requests for *baptism, promised to return later. The missionary schooner *Pitcairn* reached the island in 1890, after which most of the islanders were baptized. The vessel eventually made six missionary voyages before it was sold.

plain teaching. Although Ellen G. White never used the term *plain reading*, she did however use the term *plain teaching* to indicate the *perspicuity, or clarity, of Scripture, which is one of the great teachings of the *Protestant Reformation. Although God's *revelation is full of mystery because a full understanding of God is beyond human comprehension, there are certain things that are clearly revealed. Most obvious is God's *love, which is "made plain" for human beings (Ed 16).

plaudit. Praise (4T 413).

popish. Pertaining to the Roman Catholic Church, and in particular, the Roman Catholic curia or papacy. This term is often used to refer to the papacy's tendency through the centuries to assert his primacy and authority over others and above the Word of God. In this sense, Ellen G. White warns against "popish superstition" and "popish rites" (GC 195, 235).

porridge. Cooked cereal, often as breakfast food. "Grains used for porridge or 'mush' should have several hours' cooking" (MH 301).

positive. Ellen G. White used the term in such phrases as "positive temperament" to mean a dogmatic or overly confident opinion (3T 536; cf. 3T 533). *See also* temperament.

practical godliness/religion. A term used in various forms to describe the practical implementation of *truth in the life of the believer. It is not enough to merely assent theoretically; the message of truth must change one's behavior, otherwise it is useless. The best example of practical godliness is found in "the life of Christ and His lessons" (3T 214).

prayer. Ellen G. White described prayer as "the opening of the heart to God as to a friend" (4T 533). Prayer is an act of worship. "God hears prayer," she wrote (MH 226). The *Bible should never be studied without a "prayerful dependence upon God" (GC 599). God wants us to wrestle with Him in prayer (COL 232). "Prayer unites us with one another and with God. Prayer brings Jesus to our side, and gives to the fainting, perplexed soul new strength to overcome the world, the flesh, and the devil. Prayer turns aside the attacks of Satan" (COL 250). When our prayers are not answered or are not answered in the way we prefer, God may be testing us or may be planning to do something better for us than we can imagine. "God is too wise and good to answer our prayers always at just the time and in just the manner we desire" (MH 231). Similarly, if Christians see that "persons are not raised to health [even when prayed for], they should not on this account be judged as wanting in faith" (MH 230). Ellen G. White also warned that "prayer is not an expiation for sin; it has no virtue or merit of itself" (MB 86). The Pharisees' lengthy prayers are examples of the "outworking of the principle of self-expiation which lies at the foundation of all systems of false religion." Such a "pagan idea of prayer" exists among Christians who repeat "set, customary phrases, when the heart feels no need of God" (MB 86).

preaching. The *work of the gospel minister through the preaching of the *Bible is a sacred and holy work. The earliest Sabbatarian Adventist ministers were largely itinerant and functioned primarily as evangelists. With few ministers available, they could, at best, only visit most churches periodically to conduct the *Lord's Supper or officiate at *baptisms. Church members should not necessarily expect a sermon every week (7T 19). When the congregants were fortunate enough to hear such a sermon, those who listened were to have open hearts—no matter how flawed the messenger and the delivery of the message—for a word of *truth in which they could discern truth that applied to their own lives. While church members should use common sense, Ellen G. White considered it a grave sin to exhibit *faultfinding with the delivery of the message. She furthermore encouraged ministers to be diligent to improve their gift through careful Bible study and delivery. The most important preparation is to make sure that the preacher, through *prayer and heart searching, wrestles with the Word of God. As the preacher's heart is convicted, he or she will become a "living epistle" that will have greater impact upon listeners (5T 386). Every sermon preached is a sacred act and an opportunity to invite someone to accept Jesus Christ as Savior. "No discourse should ever be preached without presenting Christ and Him crucified as the foundation of the gospel" (GW 158).

Preble, Thomas M. (1810–1907). A Millerite and an early proponent of the seventh-day *Sabbath. His article and tract were instrumental in the acceptance of the seventh-day Sabbath by *Joseph Bates, *J. N. Andrews, and James and

Ellen G. White. He later renounced the seventh-day Sabbath.

preceptor or preceptress. Dean of men or women at a school, respectively.

prejudice. Ellen G. White lived during a turbulent time, particularly in the years leading up to the American Civil War (1861–1865), due to the issue of slavery. She was an ardent abolitionist. During the Reconstruction period, she worked to lessen racial prejudice and strongly supported the *Oakwood Industrial School as a school for black Americans. As Christians, we should put aside racial, socioeconomic, nationalist, and any other barriers through which people demean others. "Christ tears away the wall of partition," she wrote, "the self-love, the dividing prejudice of nationality, and teaches a love for all the human family" (MB 42).

Prescott, William Warren (1855–1944). Minister, educator, and administrator. From 1885 to 1944, he occupied many leadership positions. He served as a member of the General Conference Executive Committee for forty-two years. A talented researcher, he assisted Ellen G. White in obtaining historical sources for the 1911 edition of *The Great Controversy*. After her death, he played a leading role in the *1919 Bible Conference.

presentiment. A previous conception, sentiment, or opinion; an apprehension of something future (PP 451).

present truth. The idea that God reveals new *truth to His people that is especially relevant for them at that time. Early Sabbatarian Adventists embraced a dynamic concept of present truth. Whereas God's Word is revealed, a clearer and growing appreciation of the *character of God and the *moral government of God will continue to unfold throughout eternity. Even Jesus, as a human here on Earth, was "constantly growing in grace and in a knowledge of truth" (Ed 107). The Christian life is to be one of "constant advancement" (Ed 106). Ellen G. White also emphasized that "in every generation God has a special truth and a special work" (COL 78).

Preston, Rachel (Harris) Oakes (1809–1868). Seventh Day Baptist who later became a Seventh-day Adventist. During the *Millerite revival, she shared her convictions about the seventh-day *Sabbath with Frederick Wheeler, her minister, who presumably shared his views with *T. M. Preble, another nearby minister.

probation/probationers. The time granted to each individual to prepare for eternity (4T 147). The close of probation occurs either when a person dies, or (for those who are alive) just before the *second coming of Jesus Christ and is followed immediately by the time of trouble.

profligate. A licentious, dissolute individual who is excessively wasteful. Ellen G. White used this term to describe King Solomon as part of his spiritual decline (PK 58).

progress. The "spirit of progress" is a characteristic of the Christian life. "We must guard continually against being fixed in our views, feelings, and actions. The work of God is onward. Reforms must be carried on, and we must take hold and help move on the car [train] of reform" (3T 540). Antebellum America is generally characterized by most historians as the great age of reform movements.

promiscuous. A term during Ellen G. White's lifetime that referred to mingling or associating; it has nothing to do with the modern sexual connotation. For example, she frequently refers to the "promiscuous throng" or "promiscuous multitude" who listened to Jesus (DA 154, 267; MH 75).

propensity/propensities. Ellen G. White described human beings as having "inclinations and propensities" toward sin (4T 215).

prophecy, gift of. According to 2 Timothy 3:16, "all Scripture [*pasa graphē*] is God-breathed" (NIV). This means that the entire *Bible is inspired and that no part is more or less inspired. In the same way, God inspires individuals (2 Peter 1:21). Some examples of biblical prophets include Balaam who delivered oracles (Numbers 23, 24); David, who said that "the Lord spoke by me, and His word was on my tongue" (2 Samuel 23:2, NKJV); and noncanonical prophets, such as Huldah, who was just as inspired as her contemporary Jeremiah. Thus, prophets act as a mouthpiece for God. Ellen G. White never claimed to be a prophet. When someone queried her on this point, she responded,

> I have had no claims to make, only that I *am instructed that I am the Lord's messenger*; that He called me in my youth to be His messenger, to receive His Word, and to give a clear and decided message in the name of the Lord Jesus.
>
> Early in my youth I was asked several times, Are you a prophet? I have ever responded, I am the Lord's messenger. I know that many have called me a prophet, but I have made no claims to this title (1SM 32; emphasis in the original).

Ellen G. White appears to have resisted modern connotations of the term *prophet* while she had no problem with the biblical role of a prophetic messenger.

prophet, tests of a. The *gift of prophecy is a spiritual gift from the *Holy Spirit. Seventh-day Adventists believe that all claims to the prophetic gift should be evaluated by faithfulness to the teachings of Scripture. While their source (*revelation) and communication (*inspiration) are the same as Scripture, all postbiblical revelations are considered to be subject to the *authority of Scripture. Scripture warns against false prophets, so Christians must beware of them (MB 145, 146). A true prophet will profess the divine-human nature of Jesus Christ; the prophet's predictions will come true; and the prophet's life will be lived in a manner that is consistent with his or her teachings and that bears spiritual fruit (the orchard test).

propriety. Conformity to socially accepted standards of behavior. Children should be taught the rules of propriety (CG 101). Ministers are especially admonished about their need to set an example of "order" and "propriety" in their personal appearance (2T 610). Similarly, women should never be lured away from the strictest propriety (TSB 243). Ultimately, "love imparts to its possessor grace, propriety, and comeliness of deportment" (4T 559; MH 490).

proslavery men. As the American Civil War (1861–1865) progressed, Ellen G. White warned against certain "proslavery men" and "traitors" in the *North who were sympathizers with "the South" (1T 268). They were often called "Copperheads" in the newspapers.

Protestant. A reference to the religious upheaval of the sixteenth century that led to the Reformers' "protest" against the abuses of the Roman Catholic Church. Ellen G. White called for Seventh-day Adventists to uphold the same principle of *sola scriptura*, or the *Bible alone*, as its great

Protestant heritage. We have a responsibility to continue to defend it until the *second advent of Christ (6T 402, 403).

protracted meeting. A religious meeting typically lasting several days. The term took on significance in the 1830s during the Second Great Awakening. Ellen G. White generally referred to a "protracted meeting" by other denominations, although other early Adventist pioneers used the term.

psychology. Ellen G. White warned that the "sciences of phrenology, psychology, and *mesmerism" are tools used by Satan to deceive (1T 290). These were each broad terms used to describe any and all practices associated with the brain, and they should not be confused with the modern scientific study of psychology.

public house. A *Victorian term used to describe an inn with a bar or saloon, sometimes abbreviated as a "pub" (MH 338). Such places frequently offered lodging (LS80 250).

Puritan/Puritanism. A group of English Reformed Protestants from the sixteenth and seventeenth centuries who sought to reform the Church of England. The Puritan revival of the seventeenth century in Europe culminated with efforts to carry out its reforms while under *persecution. Early settlements in New England were dominated by the Puritans as they sought to mold society after their ideals. Early New England was heavily influenced by Puritan thinking, and by extension, early Adventism was influenced by Puritan thinking. Most noticeable was the early observance of the seventh-day *Sabbath that reflected in many ways the strict practice of Sunday observance by the Puritans.

pygmies. A reference to people groups of short stature. Ellen G. White makes a passing reference to such short individuals in *Patriarchs and Prophets* (436).

Q

quay. A concrete, stone, or metal platform associated with the docking of ships (GC 305).

quit themselves like men. An expression that indicates a resolute determination and fearlessness (MH 136).

R

Radical Reformation. A series of "radical" Reformers urged that the *Protestant Reformation under *Martin Luther, *John Calvin, and others had not gone far enough to instill the purity of the New Testament *church. They emphasized the need, for example, to avoid infant *baptism and that only adult believers who were converted should be fully baptized by immersion. Some radical Reformers called for the observance of the seventh-day *Sabbath. Later descendants of the Radical Reformation contributed to the nineteenth-century restorationist movement that influenced early Sabbatarian Adventist theology.

rapping. *See* Rochester rapping.

rectitude. Morally correct behavior or thinking; *righteousness. Ellen G. White used it most often in such phrases as "path of rectitude" or "inward rectitude." "Rectitude in all things is essential to the welfare of the soul" (YI Sept. 12, 1901).

redeem. The idea of saving or being saved. Ellen G. White used it most often in such phrases as "redeem the past" or "redeem the time" (2T 155, 176, 562, 620).

redemptive history. Early Adventists believed in a historicist approach to worldly history, including Bible prophecy—God interacts with humanity and is actively involved in human history. The ultimate purpose of these interactions is the restoration of humanity. Therefore all human history is the story of redemptive history or the *great controversy conflict between Christ and Satan. The grand conclusion is the restoration of fallen humanity with the final eradication of sin.

reform. *See* progress.

Reformation, Protestant. *See* Protestant.

reform dress. A style of *dress reform popular during the late 1860s and early 1870s. This pattern was a helpful start to replace tight corsets, hooped skirts, and long dresses that got dirt and dung on them from the muddy streets (2SM 473–479). The dress was loose fitting, allowing free movement to breathe and the blood to circulate. Eventually, fashion changed in favor of garments that Adventist women could wear without compromising principle. Later in life Ellen G. White rebuked some women who advocated a return to this specific style of clothing.

religious exercises. A general term to describe a religious meeting.

remnant people. Ellen White used the term *remnant* in a theological way to describe those who were faithful to God during times of crisis throughout history (PK 333, 376, 426; AA 376, 377). Literally, *remnant* means the "last part." One will find most of Ellen White's uses of the term in the context of events related to the nature, mission, and experience of the end-time people of God. She used Revelation 12:17 and 14:12 to describe the remnant as those who have the patience of the saints, keep the commandments of God, and have the testimony and faith of Jesus (TM 58; ST Nov. 1, 1899; RH July 28, 1904). While she believed that the *Adventist movement is the only one to meet this particular description (LDE 43), she did not conclude that the people of God are found exclusively in the Adventist Church (GC 383). Nevertheless, she believed that the end-time remnant embodied the Adventist movement for a particular divine purpose. It is to be a reform movement within Christianity that calls for the restoration of truths rejected or ignored by professed believers (CC 269; CD 36).

renovation. Another term for *revival (DA 406).

repentance. *Repentance* is the turning away from sin that leads to a change of heart, described as *conversion. "Repentance is turning from self to Christ," commented Ellen G. White (MB 87). Repentance entails a deep mourning over sin. The *Bible states that it is "the goodness of God" that ultimately leads a person to repentance (Romans 2:4).

reproof(s)/faithful reproof. Ellen G. White urged the biblical example of reproof that should begin with "mild measures," followed by more stern measures to warn others about *character defects (4T 517).

revelation and inspiration. *Revelation* is the idea that God communicates with human beings. There are two types of revelation: *general revelation through *nature, despite being marred by sin; and *special revelation that takes place through the direct influence of the *Holy Spirit. This latter form of revelation commonly occurs through special spokespersons known as prophets and occurs in both oral and written forms. Closely connected to revelation is *inspiration*—the divine process in which God enabled the prophets to communicate the content of revelation in a trustworthy and reliable way. Ellen G. White thus viewed the *Bible as the revealed will of God and the prophets as His inspired spokespersons. She understood inspiration as influencing the whole person and not just the words. As such, her understanding of inspiration focused more on the thoughts of the prophet rather than his or her words, although it included both (1SM 15–18).

R

Review and Herald. The main publication of Sabbatarian Adventists; it was combined from the *Present Truth* and **Advent Review* in 1850. The name of the publication went through several different forms, but they all included the main title *Review and Herald.*

revival. A revival implies an earlier period of renewal. Millerite Adventists were a part of the Second Great Awakening—a series of religious revivals across America, particularly from the 1820s up through the early 1840s. Later, Seventh-day Adventists experienced several significant revivals: most notably the 1867 revival in Washington, New Hampshire, and the 1873 revival in Battle Creek, Michigan. At the *General Conference Session of 1888, Ellen G. White praised the revival message of *E. J. Waggoner and *A. T. Jones. She believed that their revival message was the beginning of the *latter rain and loud cry that would help to prepare God's people for the *Second Coming. Opposition to this revival message by some Adventist ministers and administrators was one of the most difficult experiences of her life. Ellen G. White regularly called for spiritual revival but noted that such revival experiences must be accompanied by reformation, or changes that are implemented in the experience of believers.

rich repast. A feast (MH 47), either physically or spiritually.

righteousness. A theological term for rightdoing. Ellen G. White stated, "The essence of all righteousness is loyalty to our Redeemer" (COL 97). She distinguished between "imputed" righteousness (justification) and "imparted" righteousness (*sanctification). "The first is our title to heaven, the second is our fitness for heaven" (RH June 4, 1895).

righteousness by faith. The concept that people are saved by *faith in Jesus Christ as their Savior as opposed to earning salvation through works. Ellen G. White strongly affirmed the role of *Martin Luther and the *Protestant Reformation with their emphasis upon righteousness by faith. During her lifetime, she saw the *church move toward legalism. The church had become as "dry as the hills of Gilboa" spiritually (RH Mar. 11, 1890). She strongly supported the emphasis upon Christ and His righteousness as taught by *A. T. Jones and *E. J. Waggoner at the *General Conference Session of 1888.

rill. A tiny flow of water that often leads to a small stream (Ed 116).

"Rivulet Society." In the nineteenth century, "Rivulet Societies" were organized to help raise funds for the translation of the Bible. Ellen White affirmed those who in *Sabbath Schools raised funds for such purposes (ST May 4, 1888).

Robinson, Asa Theron (1850–1949). Minister and administrator. In 1876, he married Loretta Farnsworth (1857–1933), and in 1882, they became colporteurs. Asa was ordained in 1886, and the Robinsons went to South Africa in 1891 and to Australia after 1898. In 1903, they returned to the United States, where Asa served in a variety of administrative posts.

Rochester rapping. A series of "rappings," or noises, that the Fox sisters—Leah (1831–1890), Margaret (1833–1893), and Kate (also called Catherine) (1837–1892)—claimed to experience in their home at Hydesville, east of Rochester, New York. The two younger sisters used these rappings to convince their older sister that they were communicating with spirits. Ellen G. White considered this "mysterious rapping" as "not the result of human trickery or cunning, but was the direct work of evil angels, who thus introduced one of the most successful of soul-destroying delusions" (GC 553). Later on, the Fox sisters admitted that they made up the whole thing.

Romish. Of or pertaining to the Roman Catholic Church, which Ellen G. White believed represented a false system of worship. "The great error of the Romish Church," she counseled, "is found in the fact that the Bible is interpreted in the light of the opinions of the 'fathers.' Their opinions are regarded as infallible, and the dignitaries of the church assume that it is their prerogative to make others believe as they do, and to use force to compel the conscience" (FE 308). *See also* popish.

Rowen, Margaret Matilda (Wright) (1881–1955). Adventist convert (1912) who claimed to have the prophetic gift. She claimed her first vision occurred on June 22, 1916, less than a year after Ellen G. White's death. After an investigation, church leaders urged caution. On November 15, 1919, she was disfellowshiped from the South Side Seventh-day Adventist Church in Los Angeles, California. She announced in November 1923 that the close of *probation would occur on February 6, 1924, and that Christ would come on February 6, 1925. Her sensational announcement made newspaper headlines. Later she was caught up in a lurid murder trial, incarcerated in San Quentin State Prison, released on good behavior after a year, fled while on parole, and disappeared from public life. She sought refuge in Florida and later returned to California, where she used her maiden name and attracted a small following.

S

Sabbatarian Conferences. A series of Bible conferences held from 1848 to 1850. By the time these *conferences occurred, Adventist positions on the seventh-day *Sabbath, the state of the dead, the *Second Advent, and the *sanctuary had already been formulated, but what was truly significant was how they integrated these beliefs together into a coherent system of faith. This loose coalition of Sabbatarian Adventists coalesced into a movement that by 1860 took the name *Seventh-day Adventist* and by 1863 had organized into a General Conference.

Sabbath. Ellen G. White accepted the seventh-day Sabbath after initially resisting the idea as presented by *Joseph Bates. After her own study of the *Bible, she received a vision in which she saw a halo surrounding the fourth commandment on the tablets of stone, which were in the ark of the covenant (EW 32, 33). Ellen G. White encouraged people to make the Sabbath a meaningful time to worship God, including spending time in *nature (COL 25).

sanctification. *Sanctification* is the outworking of *grace in the life of the believer. Such outward fruits must first be preceded by God's *love (4T 610). *See also* character.

sanctuary. The biblical *doctrine of the sanctuary belongs at the heart of *Seventh-day Adventist theology. It is a prominent feature of the life and writings of Ellen G. White. Like many Millerites, she believed, based upon the day-year principle for the twenty-three hundred days of Daniel 8:14, that the sanctuary to be cleansed was this earth at the *second coming of Jesus Christ. She believed that the twenty-three hundred days began in 457 B.C. and terminated, based upon the Karaite calendar, on October 22, 1844. Soon afterward, *Hiram Edson, *O. R. L. Crosier, and Dr. F. B. Hahn studied the Bible to understand their disappointment and came to the conclusion that the sanctuary to be cleansed was in heaven, not on earth. Two of Ellen G. White's earliest visions confirm this position. In her first vision (December 1844), she received confirmation that their understanding of Bible prophecy was the beginning of a pathway; in a subsequent vision, she was shown that the Father and Son had moved to the Holy of Holies in the heavenly sanctuary. "The subject of the sanctuary," she observed years later, "was the key which unlocked the mystery of the disappointment of 1844. It opened to view a complete system of truth, connected and harmonious, showing that God's hand had directed the great advent movement and revealing present duty as it brought to light the position and work of His people" (GC 423).

scholar. *Victorian expression for "student." Ellen G. White counseled teachers to be patient with "dull scholars" (4T 420).

school home. A dormitory. Ellen G. White admonished that boarding students "should be taught that they are not independent atoms, but that each one is a thread which is to unite with other threads in composing a fabric" (6T 172). Thus, students should be given responsibilities that teach them to become dependable and productive members of society.

Second Advent/Coming. The Second Coming refers to the literal, personal return of Christ to earth with His angels in great glory to deliver His people and resurrect the righteous dead (DA 632). Also referred to as the Second Advent (arrival). This pervasive theme in Ellen White's writings left no part of her thinking unaffected. Some of her most eloquent and inspiring prose was written in connection with the events surrounding the second coming of Christ (EW 285–298; GC 635–652).

secret prayer. Private prayer that is done alone. Ellen G. White noted that "secret prayer" is vital to the Christian experience, for it "is the life of the soul" (CSA 27).

secret vice. *See* vice.

sedulous. Showing dedication and diligence (PP 729).

self. A term used to describe human nature. Ellen G. White repeatedly admonished that "self" should "be hid in Christ" (4T 613). In contrast, she warned, "To live for self is to perish" (COL 259). *See also* self-denial.

self-abuse. *See* solitary vice.

self-denial. The ability "to rule the spirit when passion is seeking for the mastery" (4T 521). "The most difficult sermon to preach and the hardest to practice is self-denial" (RC 232).

self-esteem. A term used 341 times in the published writings of Ellen G. White to describe selfishness and/or someone who is full of self-love. This selfish disposition was a *vice.

S

self-murder. A term used by Ellen G. White to indicate suicide (PP 682).

self-respect. A term used 215 times in the published writings of Ellen G. White; it is associated with human dignity and moral purity (AH 404, 426).

sentimentalism. A term used in the nineteenth century to describe an abounding expression of sentiment or opinions, or being able to quickly express intellectual feeling (PP 594).

serried. An adjective indicating rows of people or things standing close together. Ellen G. White described the "serried ranks" of Satan's host at the end of the millennium who will wage war against Jesus and God's people who are safely in the New Jerusalem (GC 664).

Seventh-day Adventist theology. Seventh-day Adventist theology formed during the 1840s after the Millerite *Great Disappointment. The central unifying theme was the *second coming of Christ. During the *Millerite revival, a number of people accepted the seventh-day *Sabbath; the most notable person was Frederick Wheeler, who learned about the seventh-day Sabbath from *Rachel Oakes Preston in Washington, New Hampshire. A short time later *T. M. Preble shared his views in an article and a tract that influenced *Joseph Bates, who shared his newfound belief with James and Ellen G. White. After the Great Disappointment, *Hiram Edson, with *O. R. L. Crosier and Dr. F. B. Hahn, studied about the *sanctuary ministry of Jesus Christ as part of the misunderstanding, which led them to explain their disappointment. The core *doctrines of the seventh-day Sabbath, sanctuary, and the Second Coming converged. Later a theology of spiritual gifts (as manifested through the prophetic ministry of Ellen G. White) and the doctrine of the nonimmortality of the soul came during a series of *Sabbatarian Conferences from 1848 to 1850. A prominent theme was the *great controversy conflict that provided a unifying eschatological foundation. By the early 1850s, Sabbatarian Adventists had developed a coherent and distinctive theological framework.

shafts. Another term for arrows or the bodies of arrows. Ellen G. White referred to the "shafts of Satan" (PP 751).

sharper. Someone who cheats (4T 617).

shipwreck. One of the most common terms to describe loss or destruction, such as making a "shipwreck of faith" (AA 76).

shock. An earthquake (GC 304, 305).

shut door. A biblical expression from Matthew 25:10 and Revelation 3:7 that the Millerites applied to the close of human *probation just before Christ's *second coming. Thus believers felt that the door of probation closed on

October 22, 1844. After the *Great Disappointment, the movement divided into two branches. The first group spiritualized away the Second Coming. A second and much smaller group of shut-door Adventists continued to believe in the prophetic significance of October 22, 1844. This latter group became known as shut-door or Bridegroom Adventists, and later Sabbatarian Adventism emerged from these believers. In this sense, the "shut door" represented their faith in the 1844 midnight cry.

sin. *Sin* is any form of evil that is the transgression of God's law. "Sin is the greatest of all evils" (COL 387). It originated with Satan's rebellion in heaven. The actual origin of sin is a mystery "too deep for the human mind to explain, or even fully to comprehend" (SC 106). Sin began on Earth with the fall of Adam and Eve in the Garden of Eden. Satan misrepresented God's *character as "severe and tyrannical" (GC 500; cf. MB 31). As a result, human minds have been perverted by sin. "For earth's sin and misery the gospel is the only antidote" (MH 141). "Every sin cherished," warned Ellen G. White, "weakens the character and strengthens habit," thus lessening the ability "to distinguish between right and wrong" (COL 281).

sitz bath. An antebellum expression for a bath taken by sitting in water up to one's hips. These baths were often used to relieve discomfort or pain in the lower abdomen. The bath could be either warm or hot, and substances including salts, baking soda, and vinegar were often used to relieve itching, hemorrhoids, and genital problems. During Ellen G. White's lifetime, it was believed that sitz baths relieved inflammation and constipation. Ellen G. White was known to occasionally partake of a sitz bath (see her diary entry for January 8, 1868, in Ms 12, 1868).

slave power. The social, economic, and political influence that slaveholders exerted in the *South and on the federal government during the decades prior to the American Civil War. Ellen G. White referred to this term in her writings during the war (1T 264; RH Aug. 27, 1861).

slip. A term used to refer to a bench (1T 656).

Smith, Annie Rebekah (1828–1855). Editor, poet, and hymn writer. With her brother *Uriah Smith, she experienced the *Great Disappointment. After this, she was no longer interested in Adventism. Reconverted by *Joseph Bates in 1851, she joined the **Review and Herald* staff a short time later. While the Whites traveled, she was left in charge of press operations. She tragically died from tuberculosis at the age of twenty-seven.

Smith, Uriah (1832–1903). Minister, editor, and educator. Converted with his sister *Annie Smith, he joined the **Review and Herald* staff in Rochester, New York. He later became the editor of the *Review and Herald*, a position he held for almost fifty years. Smith is perhaps best known for his writings on Bible prophecy, especially his *Thoughts, Critical and Practical, on the Book of Daniel* and *Thoughts, Critical and Practical, on the Book of on Revelation* (which were eventually compiled into a single volume in 1882). Smith was a close friend of James and Ellen G. White and, at times, was the recipient of some of her *reproofs. Although they experienced conflict, he ultimately conceded and benefited from her reproof. He became a staunch defender of her prophetic ministry. Perhaps the greatest test came in conjunction with the *General Conference Session of 1888. Ellen G. White admonished him for having a critical attitude, which he subsequently repented of and admitted to being on the wrong side.

social meeting. A social meeting was an integral part of early Seventh-day Adventist worship. Such meetings were best when all participated and *testimonies were short and frequent (GW 171). A social meeting was often interspersed with hymn singing and Bible study.

solicitude. Carefulness; concern; anxiety; uneasiness of mind occasioned by fear of evil or the desire for good (AA 201). Ellen G. White noted how some people "felt little solicitude" (PP 636).

S

solitary vice. A term used to indicate sexual addictions, especially masturbation. Ellen G. White wrote sternly against any and all forms of solitary vice (2T 390–411). Unlike other health reformers of her time, who suggested harsh physical restraints and even castration, Ellen G. White recommended that parents talk with their children about purity and make dietary changes to help resolve this problem.

soteriology. *See* justification by faith; sanctification.

South. A reference, particularly during the American Civil War (1861–1865), to the slave-holding Confederate States of America, which consisted of the governments of eleven Southern states that seceded from the Union (1860–1861) and that carried on all the affairs of a separate government and conducted a major war until defeated in the spring of 1865 (see 1T 253–268).

special revelation. *See* Bible.

speculation. The nineteenth century was rampant with various get-rich-quick schemes, such as patent rights (3T 400). Ellen G. White was not against creativity and developing new inventions (as evidenced by her support for C. A. White's combined laundry washer and wringer), but she warned against the numerous charlatans traveling around America who were looking for potential investors in an idea that had yet to be patented. Ellen G. White warned against them because people lost money on these get-quick-rich schemes, along with the loss of emotional energy as well as developing an addiction toward getting rich. Those who engaged in such things placed "themselves on the enemy's ground, subject to great temptations, disappointments, trials, and losses" (4T 617). A much wiser investment was to lay up treasure in heaven. For those who had extra money, Ellen G. White encouraged them to take "stock" by making these funds available to expand church institutions. In her early life, this meant the *Health Reform Institute or one of the publishing houses; even in her later years, she solicited funds for hospitals and churches.

spirit(s). A term sometimes used to denote a person's disposition, such as whether someone is happy or sad. At other times, Ellen G. White warned against evil spirits in the nineteenth-century *spiritualism movement.

***Spirit of Prophecy* series.** A series of four volumes published between 1870 and 1884 that expanded the earlier **Spiritual Gifts* series that expounded upon the biblical and historical narrative related to the *great controversy theme.

***Spiritual Gifts* series.** A series of four volumes published between 1858 and 1864. It was the earliest exposition of the *great controversy theme after Ellen G. White's far-reaching great controversy vision of 1858. The volumes were later expanded into the **Spirit of Prophecy* series of volumes and ultimately the *Conflict of the Ages series.

spiritualism. Ellen G. White considered all communication with Satan and his angels as evil and a form of spiritualism. The movement known as Modern Spiritualism began in 1848 with the mysterious spirit *rapping in Hydesville, New York, and flourished during the 1850s. It continued throughout the rest of the nineteenth century and found new forms of expression in the twentieth and twenty-first centuries. Ellen G. White described the rise of these spirit manifestations as an eschatological marker denoting the imminent *second advent of Christ. She compared the "magicians of heathen times" as equivalent to "spiritualistic mediums, clairvoyants, and the fortune-tellers of today" (AA 290). Similarly, she warned that none need be deceived by the lies of spiritualism because "God has given . . . sufficient light . . . to discover the snare." She noted that spiritualism, at its core, "is at war with the plainest statements of Scripture." Such communication with the dead, she observed, is "expressly forbidden" in Scripture (GC 556). "Satan has long been preparing for his final effort to deceive the world. . . . Little by little he has prepared the way for his masterpiece of deception in the development of spiritualism. He has not yet reached the full accomplishment of his designs; but it will be reached in the last remnant of time" (GC 561). "Except those who are kept by the power of God, through faith in His word, the whole world will be swept into the ranks of this delusion" (GC 562). (See Jud Lake, *A Nation in God's Hands*, Chapter 13: "Officers and the Spirits.")

spirituality. Spirituality for Ellen G. White was an essential part of the Christian experience. She most often referred to *spirituality* as communion with Christ that entails daily Bible study, *prayer, and *meditation. Such spiritual disciplines provide "fresh inspirations" for the inner life (5T 161).

S

state agent. The leader who coordinated the publication of denominational literature through the state *conference, typically through the *tract society, and directs the colporteurs in selling that literature.

stereotyped. Copied. The stereoview was a technique created to give the illusion of depth through binocular vision. The typical method was to present two offset images separately to the viewer's left eye and right eye to create depth perception. The two images were identical; thus, Ellen G. White's expression meant that something was exactly copied, or "stereotyped."

stewardship. Ellen G. White urged faithful Christian stewardship of believers' whole lives. This involves one's time and all resources, including finances. Christians should be careful not to waste such resources. "We are to save, that we may give," she observed (MH 206). In another place, she stated that "to give is to live" (COL 86, 87). The principle of liberality is such that humans should give "wherever the cause of God or the needs of humanity demand our aid" (COL 85, 86). "There is no sin in being rich if riches are not acquired by injustice" (COL 266). "Money cannot be carried into the next life; it is not needed there; but the good deeds done in winning souls to Christ are carried to the heavenly courts" (COL 266).

stoic/stoical. A generic reference to the Stoics or their *doctrines. In antebellum America, this was a common term to refer to someone who was not affected by passion or feeling or who manifested indifference to pleasure or pain. Ellen G. White encouraged people to be faithful in proclaiming the *truth, even if some who listen manifest "stoical indifference" at the peril of their very souls (1MCP 35).

stolid. Being calm and dependable; showing little emotion or animation. Ellen G. White described people who "may appear stoical and stolid. But under the ministration of the Holy Spirit, the stupidity that makes their uplifting appear so hopeless will pass away" (MH 169).

stupor. Mental insensibility or a state of near unconsciousness. Ellen G. White, for example, noted how she tried to rouse the *church from a "stupor and deathlike slumber" in describing the spiritual state of the church at the time (RH Dec. 18, 1888).

subsidence. The gradual sinking of a piece of land. Ellen G. White quoted from a book that described the subsidence of a *quay in conjunction with the Lisbon earthquake (GC 305).

Sunday law. During Ellen G. White's lifetime, there were a number of efforts to legislate Sunday observance (particularly in the United States, Canada, and Australia). Ellen G. White claimed that a central issue before Christ's *second advent will be the keeping of the seventh-day Sabbath versus Sunday observance. She stated that the faithful observance of the seventh-day Sabbath will be a great test of faith and will distinguish God's people. She argued that the same Roman Catholic Church that claimed the authority to change the seventh-day Sabbath to Sunday "never changes" (GC 581). Right before the end, as church and state seek to dominate *conscience, religious *persecution similar to that of the medieval period will be repeated. "The United States shall enforce Sunday observance" (GC 579). Thus, the keeping of the true "Sabbath will be the great test of loyalty" to the Creator (GC 605).

surfeited. To cause a person to desire no more of something as a result of having consumed or done it in excess (4T 609).

Sutherland, Edward Alexander (1865–1955). Educator and minister. After several years of training and teaching, Sutherland participated in the 1891 Harbor Springs, Michigan, educational convention. At this meeting, he was converted and determined to implement educational reforms. In 1892, he founded and became the principal of Walla Walla College in College Place, Washington. In 1897, he became the principal of *Battle Creek College, where he collaborated with *P. T. Magan on relocating the school. In 1904, they started a self-supporting school—the Nashville Agricultural and Normal Institute. (After 1937, its name was changed to Madison College.)

systematic benevolence. *See* benevolence.

T

Tay, John I. (1832–1892). Pioneer missionary to Tahiti, Pitcairn, and Fiji (1886–1892), where he died.

temper/temperament. Ellen G. White referred to various adjectives in conjunction with the words *temper* and *temperament* to describe different personality types (4T 255). She defined someone with a "good temper" as someone who is "kindly, cheerful, buoyant, generous, pitiful [full of pity], courteous, compassionate" (3T 420, 421). In contrast, Ellen G. White described the "decided character" and "positive [overly opinionated] temperament" of Jezebel, who controlled her husband Ahab. She described Ahab as being someone who was "easily molded" (PK 115).

temperance. A temperate person is someone who lives a

healthy and balanced lifestyle, including careful attention to the laws of health. "True temperance," Ellen G. White wrote, "teaches us to dispense entirely with everything hurtful and to use judiciously that which is healthful" (PP 562). Ellen White was well-known for her temperance speeches, especially warning against the dangers of alcohol (4T 275). "Intemperance," by way of contrast, "commences at our tables," wrote Ellen G. White (3T 563), and it reduces "vital energies." "Temperance in all things and firm denial of appetite is the only path of safety" (3T 561).

tent meeting. A term that refers to *camp meetings or evangelistic meetings.

testimony/testimonies. A term most often used for a personal expression of how God has led in the life of the believer. In the context of Ellen G. White's writings, the term is used to describe either an oral or a written admonition through the gift of prophetic *revelation and inspiration. The majority of Ellen G. White's earliest "testimonies" appear to have been mostly oral, and very few of those mailed are extant, which led to the practice of making copies of letters (2T 16). Sometimes she followed up an oral testimony with a written one (2T 569). It appears that such warnings were conditional, both for individuals as well as collectively (2T 154). She considered it a duty to write, although at other times she was "bidden to wait" before either writing or giving the *reproof (2T 154). At other times, this meant sharing only a portion of what was revealed (2T 291). She would see people in the audience whom she had seen in vision (2T 67). On several occasions, she noted that she did not rebuke individuals by name because there were unbelievers present (2T 539). Now and then it would take several attempts before she could commit on paper through *inspiration what she received through divine revelation. Sometimes she was sick and was unable to write or wrote out only a small portion under great difficulty due to health, travel, or some other circumstance (2T 431). With time, there were those *fanatics who misconstrued her writings. "Great advantage is taken of my words," she noted, "therefore I must move very cautiously" (2T 565).

theater. A hall in the nineteenth century, generally for theatrical plays, but it was often a place filled with prostitution and other types of *vice, particularly on the upper levels of the theater building. While a variety of dramatic productions might be presented, Ellen G. White strongly warned that Adventists should avoid such an atmosphere.

time of probation. A term used by Ellen G. White to indicate the finite amount of time each person has to prepare for eternity until either the close of probation just prior to the *second coming of Christ or the death of the particular individual (4T 147).

tonic bath or treatments. Ellen G. White described the use of cold and hot water treatments, or baths, as being an "excellent tonic" for the body. "Warm baths open the pores and thus aid in the elimination of impurities. Both warm and neutral baths soothe the nerves and equalize the circulation" (MH 237).

tract society. A Christian organization dedicated to the publication and distribution of literature. Seventh-day Adventists developed organizations in the nineteenth century that became the forerunner to modern Adventist Book Centers and related bookstores.

translations, Bible. Ellen G. White primarily used the King James Version during her lifetime, but she also availed herself of other Bible translations as they became available. Some of her later books, such as *Education* (1903) and *The Ministry of Healing* (1905), cite the Revised Version (1885) and American Standard Version (1901), with their marginal readings, as well as other translations, including Rotherham's Emphasized Bible (1902), the Leeser Bible (1853), and Noyes's translation (1869).

trials. The term Ellen G. White used most often to describe conflict, such as "church trials" to describe conflicted churches or "heart trials" to describe the inner human struggle. Trials, she believed, were opportunities for personal and spiritual growth (4T 354). Church trials must be dealt with (3T 10, 107), but when unnecessary should be avoided (3T 107). At least three different types of church trials can be observed in early Adventism. The first concerned localized church trials that administered the advice of Matthew 18:15–17 to resolve individual sin. The second type related to the law because early Adventists were reticent to sue one another in court (following the counsel of 1 Corinthians 6:1–8). A third kind revolved around Laodicean trials, which is a reference to the apathetic, Laodicean spiritual state of the *church (Revelation 3:14–22). This latter group was quite unique in that every church member was investigated by an itinerant minister (or two) to ascertain the *spirituality of the congregation. Following the examination, the congregation decided who would stay and who would be disfellowshiped. Afterward, the church was often reorganized by adopting a new covenant or series of resolutions.

Trinity. *See* Godhead.

true religion. A term that Ellen G. White used more than four hundred times in her published writings to contrast Bible religion with false religions. "All true religion is found" in Scripture (CT 453). "In the story of the good Samaritan, Christ illustrates the nature of true religion" (DA 497).

truth. Ellen G. White spoke a great deal about truth in the ultimate sense of divine truth. She also referred to inspired words being "cutting truth" (DA 171). She noted different sources of spiritual truth, including God's "works [nature], in His Word [Scripture], and by His providences" (COL 23). "Christ is the truth. His words are truth, and they have a deeper significance than appears on the surface. . . . Minds that are quickened by the Holy Spirit" "will discern the precious gems of truth" (COL 110).

"truth as it is in Jesus." A phrase that occurs 1,314 times in the writings of Ellen G. White. The earliest Christians witnessed about the "truth as it is in Jesus" (AA 42). All Christian theology must center upon the ultimate truth as found in the life, teachings, death, and resurrection of Jesus Christ.

U

union conferences. An intermediary level of church governance that first developed during the 1890s in Australia. It was adopted as part of the reorganization of the denomination in 1901 as an intermediate level of church governance that functioned as a check against *kingly power at the church headquarters.

unions, labor. During Ellen G. White's lifetime, labor or trade disputes were common, particularly as America moved from an agrarian to a largely urban and industrial setting. Ellen G. White viewed the mass wealth brought about through oppression as immoral, but at the same time, she also opposed labor unions that encouraged violence and other forceful tactics. She urged Adventists to avoid them. Such unions were a sign of the last days. "The trade unions," she observed, "will be one of the agencies that will bring upon this earth a time of trouble such as has not been since the world began" (4MR 88).

unsullied. Untainted. For example, Ellen G. White stated that "a character unsullied before God is rare" (4T 622).

untrammeled. Unrestricted or free to act (DA 550).

V

vacillate. To alternate or waver between different opinions or actions. Ellen G. White described Solomon's son, Rehoboam, as having received from his mother, an Ammonite, "the stamp of a vacillating character" (PK 88).

vapid. Offering nothing stimulating or of interest (DA 208).

vegetarianism. Ellen G. White was a great meat eater who, during the course of her lifetime, gradually converted to a vegetarian diet. During the 1860s, she largely gave up meat eating but continued to occasionally eat meat while she traveled. During the 1890s, she completely quit eating meat over concerns about animal cruelty. A vegetarian diet, she contended, was God's original diet for humanity in the Garden of Eden. She also warned that meat eating had a tendency to inflame the "lower propensities" of human nature (Ed 203).

vehement. Strong feelings; forceful; or showing passion (DA 254).

vice. A term used by Ellen G. White to describe sinful *habits. The word is used 671 times in her published writings; twenty-nine of those usages are directly associated with "secret vice"—an expression that describes masturbation. Within "the republican vision" of antebellum America, this term was generally "a designation for self-serving, corrupt, conspiratorial, luxurious, or venial practices that undercut freedom and destroyed social wellbeing" (Mark A. Noll, *America's God: From Jonathan Edwards to Abraham Lincoln* [New York: Oxford University Press, 2002], 568).

vicissitudes. A change of circumstances or fortune, usually in an unfortunate way (PP 471, 601, 649; Ed 164).

Victorian. A term used to describe the *Protestant middle-class culture of the latter part of the nineteenth century, largely during the reign of Great Britain's Queen Victoria (1837–1901). The term expresses society's formal reverence for its religious heritage with a deep concern for morality, respectability, and order. Victorians placed great value on both rationality and sentiment. The era was characterized by the desire for order in society, including its technology, as it was a time period noted for its use of statistics, standardization, professionalism, specialization, and tremendous industrial expansion. It was an age of print—a medium well suited to the emphasis upon permanence. Lastly, Victorians were often characterized by their emotion and romantic sentiments.

vigilant. Keeping careful watch for potential danger or difficulty.

Vigilant Missionary Society. A society founded in 1869 for the promulgation of Adventist literature and missionary work.

virtue. A term used 1,865 times in Ellen G. White's published writings to describe the three virtues of *faith, hope, and love (1 Corinthians 13:13) or the fruit of the Spirit (Galatians 5:22, 23). In a strict classical sense, Niccolò Machiavelli, in *The Prince,* styled *virtù* as manly valor displayed in defending the commonwealth; but the term later was generalized to mean disinterested service for the common good. By the early nineteenth century, the word took on a stronger female, private, and domestic sense that emphasized sexual purity. In antebellum times, most Americans had adapted the term to include a religious meaning in which "the health of a republic required the exercise of virtue by its citizens." Thus, they "defined virtue in biblical terms as life guided by God's will and cultivated in personal and domestic devotion" (Mark A. Noll, *America's God: From Jonathan Edwards to Abraham Lincoln* [New York: Oxford University Press, 2002], 90). Such a broad term masked many subtle meanings, especially spiritual nuances that included the idea that virtue must be taught and enforced. Ellen G. White used the term to emphasize a principle-based life (AH 334). Within the *Victorian context, "female virtue" indicated the principles of modesty (2T 560). In theological terms, Ellen G. White described the need "to appropriate" the "virtue of the atoning sacrifice" of Jesus Christ (PP 277). Similarly, all "healing virtue" comes from Christ (DA 471), who is the source of all true virtue (DA 92). When this same virtue enters souls, it convicts them of sin. Ellen G. White wrote, "It is the glory of God to give His virtue to His children" (AA 530).

visions and dreams. Form of *special revelation through the prophetic gift. During her lifetime, it is believed that Ellen G. White had somewhere between several hundred to as many as two thousand visions and dreams. She frequently received dramatic visions in her early prophetic ministry that began with the repetition of the word **glory* three times. Her visions and dreams were highly visual and were frequently described in terms of *light and darkness.

visual art. Ellen G. White appreciated and encouraged various forms of visual art that illustrated the biblical narrative, including prophetic charts and diagrams. In later life, she affirmed the creative use of papier-mâché depictions of the beasts in Daniel and Revelation for evangelistic meetings. At the same time, particularly during her travels through Europe (1885–1887), she noted how humans admired the achievements of great artists, but their artwork paled in comparison to the majesty and grandeur of God's actual creation.

vital. A popular reference to the vitalist theory, which had ancient roots in Egyptian and Greek philosophy, that living things inherently have a vital force, or energy, to them. A popular manifestation of this perspective was the theory of *animal magnetism. From the worldview of Ellen G. White, it was essential to not lessen one's "vital force," so believers were to live the most healthful lives possible (3T 138). She noted that "whatever hinders the circulation of the electric current in the nervous system, thus weakening the vital powers . . . makes it more difficult to arouse the moral nature" (Ed 209). She stated that "vital godliness is a principle to be cultivated" (3T 188). In the illustration about the vine and the branches, she described a personal relationship with Jesus Christ as a "vital connection" (DA

676). In this sense, every Christian must be "vitalized by divine power" (MH 56). Ellen G. White identified different sources of such "vital power," including Christ's name (AA 28), His love (MH 115), and the Word of God (AA 370). All Christians must be "vitalized by divine power" (DA 361).

vivifying. The idea of bringing to life and enlivening. Ellen G. White referred to the "vivifying power" of God (YRP 45).

vouchsafed. A term that in the nineteenth century indicated some kind of protection, especially when granted in a gracious or at times condescending manner. Thus, Ellen G. White emphasizes God's gracious character when she refers to the promises in the book of Colossians that "set forth the glorious privileges vouchsafed to the children of God" (SL 85).

W

wagon, gospel. A term used in conjunction with the wagon trains of the westward expansion and settlement of the United States. An individual wagon could take part in a wagon train, so Ellen G. White framed a spiritual analogy with similar language, such as joining a "gospel wagon." During the 1890s, as urban centers in America grew, there were conscious attempts to use "a horse-drawn wagon decorated to attract attention and moved into a city to be used as a platform from which to present the message." These gospel wagons were used by a variety of Christian groups, most notably by Dr. *J. H. Kellogg in conjunction with the Chicago Mission that he started there. Around 1899, Ellen G. White warned against large sums of money being spent on a gospel wagon ministry. While this was a noble cause, she expressed caution lest basic evangelistic needs not be met (6MR 198; 9MR 81).

Waggoner, Ellet Joseph (1855–1916). Physician and minister. After graduating from medical school in 1878, he briefly joined the staff of the *Battle Creek Sanitarium, but things did not work out. He then worked in ministry in Iowa. Ellen G. White rebuked him for his headstrong manners and inability to work well with others, which troubled his early ministry (4T 437–439). He moved to California, where he experienced a dramatic *conversion at the 1882 California camp meeting. He worked briefly at the Rural Health Retreat (later the St. Helena Sanitarium). By 1883, he switched to full-time ministerial work that included assisting his father, *J. H. Waggoner, in editing the *Signs of the Times*. *A. T. Jones joined the staff in 1885, and by mid-1886, they became coeditors. Waggoner is best known for his *revival message presented with Jones around the time of the *General Conference Session of 1888. Ellen G. White described the resistance to this message as the most difficult time period of her life. In the late 1890s, Waggoner was influenced by the *pantheism of Dr. *J. H. Kellogg. He subsequently apostatized from the denomination and left his wife to marry a nurse in England.

Waggoner, Joseph Harvey (1820–1889). Minister, editor, and missionary. He was converted in 1851 and afterward was an itinerant evangelist. In 1878, he moved to California where he became the editor of *Signs of the Times*. Ellen G. White admonished both Waggoner and his wife, Mariette (1823–1908), due to their critical spirit. At various stages in their lives, both Mariette and Joseph experienced moral failings. After Joseph had an affair with Lottie Chittenden in California, he returned to Battle Creek, Michigan. Once he had thoroughly repented, Ellen G. White encouraged him to go to Europe as a missionary. He died in 1889 and is buried next to *J. N. Andrews.

Waldenses or Waldensians. A group of ancient Christians from the Alps of northern Italy and southern France who coalesced during the medieval period. They are known for their preservation and translation of the *Bible. During the twelfth century, they became particularly well known under the reforms and leadership of Peter Waldo, a rich merchant from Lyon who adopted a strict life of simplicity and poverty. The Waldenses were excommunicated by Pope Lucius III in 1184 and faced a series of severe *persecutions. The narrative of the Waldensians occupies a prominent place in Ellen G. White's history of the *great controversy conflict between Christ and Satan during the High Middle Ages (GC 65). *See also* Albigenses.

ward. A nineteenth-century term for a section of a prison or a jail (PP 408); also a hospital ward or a political division of a city.

water treatment. Medical treatments utilizing hot and cold water as a natural remedy.

weal or woe. *Weal* means to be in a healthy, sound, or prosperous state. *Woe* means to suffer challenges, poor health, or adversity. Both terms come from an old English expression. Ellen G. White warned that one of the important lessons from Solomon's life is "the power of influence for good or for ill." She stated that each person exerts "an influence for weal or woe" (PK 85). Similarly, a proper *education "is bound up [with] life's weal or woe" (Ed 234).

Wesley, John (1703–1791). Minister and revivalist; co-founder of the *Methodist movement that was a part of the transatlantic evangelical *revival. John and his brother Charles Wesley (1707–1788) were Arminians who believed in free will, as opposed to *John Calvin's emphasis that only the elect are saved. It is difficult to overestimate the influence of Wesley and *Methodism in American religion. Methodism went from a modest movement in the mid-eighteenth century to the largest and most significant denomination in the first half of the nineteenth century. Ellen G. White grew up in a Methodist home with a strong Arminian focus. Many of her sensible values about *sanctification are a direct result of her Methodist understanding of the relationship between law and *grace. Despite the fact that Ellen and her family were disfellowshiped from the Chestnut Street *Methodist Church in Portland, Maine, for their *Second Advent views during the *Millerite revival, she appeared to have held a high regard for the core of Wesley's theology, even though she was somewhat critical of American Methodism in general. *See also* Methodism.

Western Health Reform Institute. *See* Health Reform Institute.

White, Arthur Lacey (1907–1991). Grandson of Ellen G. White, third son of *W. C. White, and secretary of the *Ellen G. White Estate Inc. (1937–1978). After the death of his father, he assisted in relocating the unpublished writings of Ellen G. White and other historical materials in the *Elmshaven vault to the General Conference headquarters in Takoma Park, Maryland. In retirement, he wrote a six-volume biography of Ellen G. White's life.

White, Ellen Gould (Harmon) (1827–1915). Visionary, church leader, and author. Ellen G. White was born on November 26, 1827, in Gorham, Maine, and died on July 16, 1915, at her *Elmshaven home in California. For a more detailed overview of her life, see the biographical introduction "Who Was Ellen G. White?"

White Estate, Ellen G., Inc. Organization that was set up at the request of the General Conference of Seventh-day Adventists to honor the wishes of Ellen G. White to create an organization, led by a board originally composed of five trustees, to preserve and promulgate her writings after her death.

White, Henry Nichols (1847–1863). Oldest son of James and Ellen G. White. Henry was named after the family's friend Henry Otis Nichols. He was born in Gorham, Maine, at a time when his parents were impoverished. Soon afterward the family moved in with Stockbridge and Louisa Howland. Ellen G. White, then nineteen years old, hoped to stay home more; but after a brief illness, she believed that God wanted her to travel and share the messages she received with the nascent Sabbatarian Adventist believers. For the first five years of his life, Henry lived with the Howland family. In 1863, after a period of spiritual renewal, Henry was baptized with a group of friends by his father, *James White, in the Kalamazoo River in Michigan. Tragically, Henry died of pneumonia on December 8, 1863, after being treated with conventional *drugs. In Ellen G. White's later years, she wished that at this early time she had known what she later did about *health reform: "If we had only known then what we know now, we could have saved Henry."

White, James Edson (1849–1928). The oldest surviving son of James and Ellen G. White, minister, and missionary.

At the age of fifteen, Edson was employed at the Review and Herald publishing *office and mastered the print trade. On July 28, 1870, he married Emma McDearmon. In April 1877, he was asked to be responsible for the newly established Pacific Seventh-day Adventist Publishing Association in California; he retained this position for three years. While there, he spearheaded the publication of the *Song Anchor*, the first Seventh-day Adventist songbook in which all the songs were set to music. In the 1880s, he became a leader in the Sabbath School movement and continued publishing various songbooks but gradually drifted away from the *church. In 1893, after a time of spiritual rekindling, Edson read a copy of his mother's tract *Our Duty to the Colored People* (1891) that included an appeal for missionary work for disenfranchised African Americans in the southern United States. He raised funds and built a missionary steamboat, the *Morning Star*, which served as a mobile base for *education, nursing, and *evangelism as he, his wife, and a group of workers traveled along the tributaries of the Mississippi River. During this time, they organized the Southern Missionary Society (1895); launched the *Gospel Herald*, a new publication (1898); and started a small printing office (1900) that ultimately became the Southern Publishing Association. In 1912, they settled in Marshall, Michigan, due to Emma's failing health. After her death in 1917, Edson relocated to Battle Creek, where he developed stereopticon slides. In 1922, he married Rebecca Burrill.

White, James Springer (1821–1881). Minister, publisher, author, and a cofounder of the Seventh-day Adventist Church. He was ordained as a Christian Connexion minister and became an itinerant Millerite preacher in Maine. After the *Great Disappointment, he met Ellen G. Harmon, became convinced of the genuineness of her visions, and assisted her in her travels. In 1846, they were married. Together they actively participated in a series of *Sabbatarian Conferences from 1848 to 1850, out of which the core theological framework of the Seventh-day Adventist Church came together. In 1848, Ellen G. White encouraged James to start publishing, which led to the publication of the *Present Truth* (1849) and the **Advent Review* (1850), which were combined into the *Review and Herald.* After a series of moves, they relocated by 1855 to Battle Creek, Michigan. Once there, James White was a dynamic powerhouse behind the development of the fledgling denomination, especially with regard to choosing a name (1860), the formation of a publishing association (1861), and the organization of a General Conference (1863), among many other various aspects. After 1855, he turned over the editorship of the *Review and Herald* to Uriah Smith but remained actively involved in its publication as well as helping to develop and promote a wide variety of other Adventist periodicals and entities. Of special note was his poor health that led him and his wife, Ellen, to seek treatment at James C. Jackson's "Our Home on the Hillside" in Dansville, New York. He afterward was a strong supporter of the Health Reform Institute, which became the *Battle Creek Sanitarium. James White was also a strong supporter of early Adventist education, not the least of which was so that his own children could benefit from the training of people such as *Goodloe Harper Bell. Tragically, James White died from malaria in 1881, which Ellen White attributed at least in part to his consistent tendency to overwork.

White, John Herbert (Sept. 20–Dec. 14, 1860). Fourth and youngest son of James and Ellen G. White. He tragically developed *erysipelas.

White, William Clarence (1854–1937). Third son of James and Ellen G. White, minister, administrator, and editor. Born in Rochester, New York, he grew up in Battle Creek, Michigan, where he attended the fledgling school started by *Goodloe H. Bell, and was baptized at the age of twelve. He started his denominational employment at the Pacific Press Publishing Association. He married Mary Kelsey in 1876, and together they prepared for missionary service by attending *Battle Creek College. He held a variety of responsible positions in the *church, such as being elected to the General Conference Executive Committee in 1883. After the death of his father in 1881, he worked closely with his mother to support her ministry until her death in 1915. He traveled with her both to Europe (1885–1887) and Australia (1891–1900). After Mary's death in 1890, he married Ethel May Lacey in Tasmania (1895). After his mother's death, he was responsible for managing her literary estate, the *Ellen G. White Estate Inc.

Wolff, Joseph (1795–1862). Missionary and author. A Jew who converted to Roman Catholicism, he eventually became a *Protestant missionary under the influence of Edward Irving. Ellen G. White regarded his missionary travels in which he promulgated his convictions about the *Second Coming as a prophetic fulfillment of a worldwide Advent awakening.

womanliness. In *Victorian America, this was a frequent reference to female *virtue. Ellen G. White counseled that young girls "should be taught that the true charm of womanliness is not alone in beauty of form or feature" but "in patience, generosity, kindness, and a willingness to do and suffer for others. They should be taught . . . to trust in God and fear Him" (CG 140). *See also* manliness.

wonted. Regular or habitual (PK 342).

work. Ellen G. White had a strong work ethic and believed that Christians should hold high, ethical work standards. At times she admonished some individuals for their laziness, and in other situations, people for workaholism. She often spoke of the "work of God" as God working through the ministry of the church, which today "extends over all the earth" (AA 337–338).

works, human. Ellen G. White repeatedly urged "the impossibility of fallen man meriting anything by his own best good works." For her, "salvation is through faith in Jesus Christ alone." "If man cannot, by any of his good works, merit salvation, then it must be wholly of grace, received by man as a sinner because he receives and believes in Jesus. It is wholly a free gift" (3MR 420). But once a person is in a right relationship with God through *justification by faith, "there is yet another work to be accomplished, and this is of a progressive nature. The soul is to be sanctified through the truth. And this also is accomplished through faith. For it is only by the grace of Christ, which we receive through faith, that the character can be transformed" (ST Nov. 3, 1890). These "good works" are the result of *sanctification and are "dependent on a power outside of ourselves" (COL 160). Thus Ellen G. White condemned human works of "creature merit" (3MR 420) but affirmed "good works" of faith through the experience of sanctification. Her emphasis was always on Christ and His righteousness rather than human works: "The proud heart strives to earn salvation; but both our title to heaven [justification] and our fitness for it [sanctification] are found in the righteousness of Christ" (DA 300).

worsted. As a noun, *worsted* is a fine, smooth yarn spun from combed long wool (e.g., a "worsted suit"). As a verb, it is used to describe someone who has been defeated, such as when *Martin Luther presented his case before the German princes. By his testimony, "the partisans of Rome had been worsted" (GC 161).

worthy poor. Some individuals who, through no fault of their own, experience misfortune and thereby significant hardship and poverty. Ellen G. White repeatedly cared for and shared her own resources—financially or by providing food and clothes. She furthermore urged that each church should have "a fund to aid such worthy poor families who love God and keep His commandments" (CCh 284).

writings, interpretation of. Ellen G. White recognized the danger of distorting her writings and enunciated principles of interpretation in order to understand her writings in a healthy and balanced way. Such principles apply similarly to the *Bible and her writings, although she recognized that the Bible, as an act of *revelation, is the final *authority. Adventist scholars have recognized eight basic hermeneutical principles. *See* introductory essay "How to Interpret Ellen G. White's Writings."

Chronology

Aug. 4, 1821	James White is born in Palmyra, Maine.
Nov. 26, 1827	Ellen G. Harmon is born near Gorham, Maine, to Robert and Eunice Harmon.
Late 1836	Ellen G. Harmon receives concussion after being struck by a rock.
Mar. 11–23, 1840	Ellen G. Harmon listens to William Miller preach in Portland, Maine.
Sept. 1841	Ellen G. Harmon attends Methodist camp meeting in Buxton, Maine.
June 26, 1842	Ellen G. Harmon is baptized by John N. Hobart in Casco Bay, in Portland, Maine.
Sept. 1842	James White begins preaching.
Sept. 2, 1843	The Harmon family is expelled from the Chestnut Street Methodist Church for their Millerite views.
Oct. 22, 1844	The Great Disappointment results when Christ does not return on this day.
Summer 1844	James and Ellen G. White first meet.

Dec. 1844	Ellen G. Harmon has her first vision in Portland, Maine.
Jan./Feb. 1845	Ellen G. Harmon presents her views for the first time in public at Megquier Hill in Poland, Maine.
Jan. 24, 1846	Ellen G. Harmon's first vision published in *The Day-Star.*
Apr. 6, 1846	First broadside published by Ellen G. Harmon, titled "To the Little Remnant Scattered Abroad."
Aug. 30, 1846	James White, age 25, marries Ellen G. Harmon, age 18.
Fall 1846	James and Ellen G. White accept the seventh-day Sabbath.
Aug. 26, 1847	Henry Nichols White is born.
1848–1850	Series of Bible Conferences to develop and expound on core beliefs of Sabbatarian Adventist movement.
July 1849	The first issue of the *Present Truth* is published.
July 28, 1849	James Edson White is born.
1851–1855	The Whites relocate to 124 Mount Hope Avenue in Rochester, New York.
Aug. 29, 1854	William Clarence White is born.
Nov. 1855	James and Ellen relocate to Battle Creek, Michigan.
Dec. 1855	*Testimony for the Church*, no. 1, is published. It is the first of what eventually became a series of nine volumes.

Dec. 1856	James and Ellen G. White visit Waukon, Iowa.
Mar. 14, 1858	Ellen G. White receives far-reaching great controversy vision in Lovett's Grove, Ohio.
May 13, 1860	The first legally organized Seventh-day Adventist Church is established in Parkville, Michigan.
Sept. 20, 1860	John Herbert White is born.
Oct. 1, 1860	The name *Seventh-day Adventist* is officially adopted in order to give a legal name to the publishing house.
Dec. 14, 1860	John Herbert White dies.
Jan. 12, 1861	Ellen G. White receives a vision about a long and expensive American Civil War.
Oct. 5–6, 1861	First state conference organized in Michigan.
May 20–23, 1863	General Conference of Seventh-day Adventists is organized.
June 6, 1863	Ellen G. White receives a comprehensive health reform vision in Otsego, Michigan.
Dec. 8, 1863	Henry White dies at the age of 16 in Topsham, Maine.
Aug. 16, 1865	James White experiences first stroke.
Fall 1865	James and Ellen G. White visit "Our Home on the Hillside" water cure run by *James Caleb Jackson in Dansville, New York.
Dec. 25, 1865	Ellen G. White receives a vision

	about the need for a health institution.
Aug. 1866	The *Health Reformer* journal begins publication.
Sept. 5, 1866	Opening of the Western Health Reform Institute.
1868	James and Ellen G. White relocate to Greenville, Michigan.
1872	The Whites make first of many trips to California.
1872–1874	James and Ellen G. White periodically take retreats to Colorado.
Apr. 1, 1874	Ellen G. White receives a vision about the need for an overseas missionary presence.
Aug. 24, 1874	Battle Creek College opens.
Jan. 3, 1875	Ellen G. White receives a vision about publishing houses around the world.
Aug. 24–29, 1876	Ellen G. White speaks to possibly her largest crowd, an estimated 20,000 people, at Groveland Camp Meeting, Massachusetts.
1878–1879	The Whites spend the winter in Texas.
Apr. 20, 1879	The Battle Creek Dime Tabernacle is dedicated.
Aug. 6, 1881	James White dies of malaria.
1885–1887	Ellen G. White goes on a missionary tour of Europe.
1886	Ellen G. White's first major statement about inspiration.

1888	Ellen G. White moves to Healdsburg, California.
Oct.–Nov. 1888	General Conference session is held in Minneapolis, Minnesota, during which Ellen G. White supports the emphasis of A. T. Jones and E. J. Waggoner on a more Christ-centered perspective of Adventist theology.
1891	Ellen G. White delivers a historic presentation entitled "Our Duty to the Colored People" at the General Conference session, appealing for the Seventh-day Adventist Church to embrace systematic outreach for black people in the South.
1891–1900	Ellen G. White works in Australia.
1892	Ellen G. White counsels Nathaniel D. Faulkhead against affiliation with secret societies.
1892	*Steps to Christ* is published by Fleming H. Revell; it is the only book to be published by Ellen G. White with a non–Seventh-day Adventist publisher.
1894	The *Morning Star* missionary boat is launched by James Edson White. The boat travels along the Mississippi River and its tributaries, and the workers aboard start schools and churches primarily for African Americans.
Dec. 25, 1895	Ellen G. White moves into

	"Sunnyside," located at Cooranbong, New South Wales, Australia.
1896	Oakwood Industrial School, now known as Oakwood University, is founded. Ellen G. White serves on the board and strongly supports this venture to educate black Americans.
Oct. 5, 1896	Ellen G. White lays cornerstone for first building at the *Avondale School, now known as Avondale College of Higher Education.
1897	Ellen G. White urges the establishment of church schools.
1898	*The Desire of Ages*, on the life of Christ, is published.
Sept. 1900	Ellen G. White purchases "Elmshaven" near St. Helena, California.
Apr. 2–21, 1901	Ellen G. White participates in church reorganization at General Conference session held at *Battle Creek, Michigan.
Summer 1901	Battle Creek College moves to Berrien Springs, Michigan, and is renamed Emmanuel Missionary College (since 1959, known as Andrews University).
Feb. 18, 1902	The Battle Creek Sanitarium is destroyed by fire.
Dec. 30, 1902	The Review and Herald publishing house is destroyed by a fire.
Oct. 1903	The General Conference

	headquarters are relocated to Takoma Park, Maryland.
1904	Ellen G. White lends her support to the founding of the self-supporting Madison College near Nashville, Tennessee.
May 26, 1905	Ellen G. White directs John Burden to purchase property in Loma Linda, California, for a medical institution.
Apr. 15, 1906	Ellen White speaks at the dedication of Loma Linda Sanitarium, located in Southern California.
May 1909	Ellen G. White attends her last General Conference session. She concludes one of her addresses by standing at the pulpit, lifting up the Bible, and challenging delegates, "I commend unto you this Book" (6BIO 197).
Feb. 9, 1912	Ellen G. White creates trusteeship for her writings.
May 1913	Ellen G. White's last messages sent to General Conference session.
June 14, 1914	Ellen G. White pens her last writings before her death.
Feb. 13, 1915	Ellen G. White breaks her hip in her Elmshaven home near St. Helena, California.
July 16, 1915	Ellen G. White dies at Elmshaven at the age of 87.
July 18, 1915	Ellen G. White's funeral is held at Elmshaven.

July 19, 1915	Another funeral is held at the Richmond, California, camp meeting.
July 24, 1915	Ellen G. White's funeral is held at the Battle Creek Tabernacle.
Dec. 1916	Ellen G. White's last book, *Prophets and Kings*, published posthumously.

Bibliography

This bibliography is not exhaustive. Instead, it lists some of the major works in each category that can serve as a useful introduction to various aspects of Ellen G. White's life and writings.

Apologetics

Brand, Leonard, and Don S. McMahon. *The Prophet and Her Critics: A Striking New Analysis Refutes the Charges That Ellen G. White "Borrowed" the Health Message.* Nampa, ID: Pacific Press®, 2005.

Fagal, William. *101 Questions About Ellen White and Her Writings*. Nampa, ID: Pacific Press®, 2010.

Lake, Jud. *Ellen White Under Fire: Identifying the Mistakes of Her Critics*. Nampa, ID: Pacific Press®, 2010.

Nichol, Francis D. *Ellen G. White and Her Critics: An Answer to the Major Charges That Critics Have Brought Against Mrs. Ellen G. White*. Washington, DC: Review and Herald®, 1951.

———. *Why I Believe in Mrs. E. G. White: Some Reasons Why Seventh-day Adventists Believe That Ellen G. White Possessed the Gift of "the Spirit of Prophecy."* Washington, DC: Review and Herald®, 1964.

Robertson, John J. *The White Truth.* Mountain View, CA: Pacific Press®, 1981.

Biographical or Introductory

Graham, Roy E. *Ellen G. White: Co-founder of the Seventh-day Adventist Church.* New York: Peter Lang, 1985.

Kaiser, Denis, and Jerry Moon. "For Jesus and Scripture: The Life of Ellen G. White." In *The Ellen G. White Encyclopedia*, edited by Jerry Moon and Denis Fortin, 18–95. Hagerstown, MD: Review and Herald®, 2014.

Knight, George R. *Meeting Ellen White: A Fresh Look at Her Life, Writings, and Major Themes.* Hagerstown, MD: Review and Herald®, 1996.

Nix, Jim. *Glimpses Into the Life of Ellen White.* Silver Spring, MD: Review and Herald®, 2016.

Noorbergen, Rene. *Ellen G. White: Prophet of Destiny.* New Canaan, CT: Keats Publishing, 1972.

Pfandl, Gerhard. *The Gift of Prophecy: The Role of Ellen White in God's Remnant Church.* Nampa, ID: Pacific Press®, 2008.

Timm, Alberto R., and Dwain N. Esmond, eds. *The Gift of Prophecy in Scripture and History.* Silver Spring, MD: Review and Herald®, 2015.

Wheeler, Ruth. *His Messenger: Best-Loved Stories of Ellen White.* Nampa, ID: Pacific Press®, 2002.

White, Arthur L. *Ellen G. White.* 6 vols. Hagerstown, MD: Review and Herald®, 1981–1986.

Hermeneutics

Burt, Merlin D., ed. *Understanding Ellen White: The Life and Work of the Most Influential Voice in Adventist History*. Nampa, ID: Pacific Press®, 2015.

Knight, George R. *Ellen White's World: A Fascinating Look at the Times in Which She Lived*. Hagerstown, MD: Review and Herald®, 1998.

———. *Reading Ellen White: How to Understand and Apply Her Writings*. Hagerstown, MD: Review and Herald®, 1997.

Read, W. E. *The Bible, the Spirit of Prophecy, and the Church*. Washington, DC: Review and Herald®, 1952.

White, Arthur L. *The Ellen G. White Writings*. Washington, DC: Review and Herald®, 1973.

Topical or Theological Studies

Coon, Roger W. *The Great Visions of Ellen G. White: Fascinating Stories Behind the Visions That Have Charted the Course of the Adventist Church*. Hagerstown, MD: Review and Herald®, 1992.

Delafield, D. A. *Ellen G. White in Europe, 1885–1887: Prepared From Ellen G. White Papers and European Historical Sources*. Washington, DC: Review and Herald®, 1975.

Gordon, Paul A. *My Dear Brother M . . . : Why Ellen White Wrote the Letters in "Testimonies for the Church."* Nampa, ID: Pacific Press®, 1997.

Hamel, Paul. *Ellen White and Music: Background and Principles*. Washington, DC: Review and Herald®, 1976.

Lake, Jud. *A Nation in God's Hands: Ellen White and the Civil War*. Nampa, ID: Pacific Press®, 2017.

Land, Gary, ed. *The World of Ellen G. White*. Hagerstown, MD: Review and Herald®, 1987.

Moon, Jerry Allen. *W. C. White and Ellen G. White: The Relationship Between the Prophet and Her Son*. Andrews University Seminary Doctoral Dissertation Series. Berrien Springs, MI: Andrews University Press, 1993.

Tutsch, Cindy. *Ellen White on Leadership: Guidance for Those Who Influence Others*. Nampa, ID: Pacific Press®, 2008.

Valentine, Gilbert M. *The Struggle for the Prophetic Heritage: Issues in the Conflict for Control of the Ellen G. White Publications, 1930–1939*. Muak Lek, Thailand: Institute Press, 2006.

———. *The Prophet and the Presidents: Ellen White's Influence on the Leadership of the Early Seventh-day Adventist Church*. Nampa, ID: Pacific Press®, 2011.

Whidden, Woodrow W. II. *Ellen White on Salvation: A Chronological Study*. Hagerstown, MD: Review and Herald®, 1995.

Reference

Fortin, Denis, and Jerry Moon, eds. *The Ellen G. White Encyclopedia*. Hagerstown, MD: Review and Herald®, 2014.